Site Guides:

Costa Rica

A Guide to the Best Birding Locations

By Dennis W. Rogers

Cover art by
Steven Heinl

For Elena Zamora,
who is Costa Rica

While every effort has been made to verify the accuracy of the information in this book, the author accepts no responsibility for any loss, inconvenience, or injury that might arise from the use of said information.

ISBN 0-9637765-2-5
Cinclus Publications
Box 284
McMinnville, OR, 97128
U.S.A.

Table of Contents

Introduction

The Pacific Lowlands

Guanacaste

The Mountains

The Atlantic Lowlands

Introduction

Costa Rica has justly gained a reputation as a birding destination, and many birders have made their first Neotropical trip to sample the varied habitats there. The small size of the country, large bird list, good field guide, and fast-developing infrastructure combine to make birding relatively easy. The friendly people and general safety of the country means birding is as comfortable as anywhere in Latin America.

Acknowledgments

This work of course could not be achieved without the help of many different people. Material by Steve Friedman, Steve Heinl, Jim Lewis, Graham Speight, Gary Stiles, and others was consulted in producing this book, especially the species lists. My thanks to them and all the others who have helped make Costa Rica a world-class birding destination.

When to Come

The best weather for birding is during the dry season from December to April. This coincides with the vacation season for the Costa Ricans, and it is very difficult to travel during the Christmas and Easter seasons. The rest of the year is rainy, though typically most precipitation comes as a cloudburst in the afternoon and doesn't affect birding too much. Be prepared for mud. On the Caribbean slope it can rain at any time.

Temperatures in the highlands are generally moderate, though it can get chilly and windy at the highest elevations. The lowlands in the dry season are hot and muggy except in Guanacaste where it is hot and dry.

International Transport

The main international airport near Alajuela is well-served from the U.S. and Canada, while continuing development in Guanacaste means the newly-expanded airport at Liberia will receive more flights. LACSA is the principle Costa Rican airline, serving New York, Miami, Orlando, New Orleans, Los Angeles, and San Francisco. It has a generally fine reputation and is a good option if you live near one of those cities. Recently Aero Costa Rica started service to Miami and Orlando and is planning routes to other cities in the U.S.

U.S. airlines serving San José include American from Miami and Dallas/Ft. Worth; Continental from Houston; and United from Miami, Washington via Mexico City, and Los Angeles via Guatemala. There are of course good connections to most cities in the U.S. from these hubs. Canadian also serves San José from Vancouver, and there are charters from eastern Canada.

Travelers from Europe can fly with Iberia or KLM but most connections are via Miami.

Other Latin American airlines also may offer good fares, though only TACA and Copa are considered very reliable. Connections to South America can be made via Panama, Venezuela, or Colombia.

It is also possible to reach Costa Rica by highway but it is not recommended unless you want to bring a vehicle to sell here (difficult but possible). The expense and hassle of crossing so many borders make this route less than worthwhile. In addition to the obvious travel expenses, you will have to pay so many fees and bribes (El Salvador and Honduras are notorious in this regard) that it can be cheaper to fly. Allow at least six days from Brownsville if you decide to drive, and don't tell the Mexicans you are going to Central America.

Domestic Flights

There is an ample schedule of domestic flights but they are not all that useful, as the birder will need transport at the end of the flight anyway and rental cars are not widely available outside San José/Alajuela. SANSA is government-owned and has a reputation for low prices and unreliability. Travelair is more reliable at higher prices. Other than a possible visit to Tortuguero with Travelair the birder should stick to the highways.

Rental Cars

The last five years have seen an explosion of small rental car companies in Costa Rica. Competition and favorable tax treatment by the government have brought prices down to the $200 per week level for a small car with unlimited milage. Four-wheel-drive can be had for as little as $280 per week. Some of the small companies are competitive but I prefer the international ones like Avis, National, Budget because when they pull something on you (highly likely) then at least you can complain at home. Be sure to reserve from outside the country for the best prices. If you have a credit card with insurance ask if you can waive the overpriced standard coverage—it is mandatory with many companies.

When you get your car be sure and check it over for scratches and dings so you don't get charged for damage that was already present. If you get a flat by all means get it fixed as the car companies may charge up to 10 times the going rate. If you want to go to Monteverde make sure your contract allows you to use that road; some don't. Others prohibit driving on any unpaved road, so a 4WD may be worth the extra money.

Gasoline prices in Costa Rica are fixed by the government, 45.1 Colons per liter for regular in early 1994. That was about $1.12 per U.S. Gallon at the time.

The worst problem with rental cars is that most have special licence plates that are an invitation to trouble from thieves and corrupt traffic police. Break-ins are a special problem around Carara and Jacó, in Braulio Carrillo, and of course in San José. Don't leave your car on the street in San José, put it in a parking lot. Don't leave anything of value in view from outside anywhere.

Many small rental cars are Japanese models with trunks which could be used to store valuables out of sight, except most now have an internal release. The thief need only break a window to have ready access to the trunk. I suggest you bring a pair of needle-nose pliers with a wire cutter and fix this problem at the latch. Don't mention this improvement to the car company though, as they tend to think all standard equipment is good.

Buses

Busses go almost anywhere you want to go in Costa Rica and they are cheap. The longest run in the country, 8 hours of pure suffering from San José to Puerto Jimenez, is only 950 Colones or $6.25. If you have the time and have no one to share costs with this is a good alternative. For specific information about schedules visit the ICT office under the Plaza de la Cultura in San José.

Driving Standards

Costa Ricans tend to lose their agreeable personalities behind the wheel of a car and that combines with the difficult roads to make driving an adventure in Costa Rica. Roads outside the central valley tend to be two lanes of asphalt (if you're lucky) with no lines or lighting. The winding roads from the valley down to the coasts and over the Cerro de la Muerte are especially difficult. Night driving is not recommended due to potholes, animals in the road, and vehicles without lights. If you need to drive at night to reach a habitat early enough in the morning, drive slowly and carefully. Some idiosyncracies of driving in San José are treated under that section.

Another problem is the traffic police, well-known for their corruption. They may seize on some real or imagined offense to try to extract a bribe from you, telling you that you have to go to some inconvenient place to pay the fine. The intersection speed zones along the freeway from the airport to San Ramón are notorious for their speed-traps. The proper thing to do is just drive away and give the ticket to your rental car company and they will pay it and add it to your bill (possibly with a surcharge). If you have been unfairly ticketed get the officer's badge number and turn that in too. Any policeman in Costa Rica must show i.d. when asked so don't let him tell you he doesn't have any. If your Spanish is up to it you can pay them off, usually waiting for the suggestion that you pay the fine now. Under no circumstances use the word "bribe" or "mordita." The going rate to fix a speeding ticket is about 1000 Colones, so don't let them bully you into more than twice that. Most of the fines are in the neighborhood of 5000 Colones so it is an economical proposition. Don't worry about corrupting the natives, due to low pay (about $250/month), poor supervision, and a general lack of professionalism, they are already corrupt.

Accommodations

Accommodation in Costa Rica runs the full gamut from first-class hotels to concrete-block hovels that suggest prison cells. San José of course has the best range but in recent years lots of places in the $30-70 range have sprung up in the countryside.

Value for money is actually similar to the U.S., though there are options at the bottom end not likely to be seen there. Generally in birding areas $30-50/night for two people will give you an ample selection. Beware some really cheap places that are also brothels (prostitution is legal in Costa Rica). Any place called a "hotel" where you can't see the parking from the road is usually a short-time place for consummating illicit affairs.

During the peak season it's probably a good idea to make reservations but not really necessary most of the year. See a good tourist guidebook and/or make reservations with the service across the street from the southeast corner of the Plaza de la Cultura in San José.

Generally I will not recommend hotels unless one is an obvious choice for birding an area. In San José you will need an upper-end place or you will have to find secure parking elsewhere. One good possibility in the $60-70 price range is the Hotel Irazú, convenient to most birding destinations around San José. A cheaper place is the San José Garden Court, though it is in the middle of one of the worst neighborhoods in San José.

Food

Cuisine is not one of Costa Rica's strong points, though "typical" food is usually good value. Rice and beans are the staple, supplemented with tough but tasty meat, vegetables, and a wide variety of fruit. Outward appearance is not a reliable measure of a restaurant, some shabby *sodas* have excellent fixed plates or *casados* while some fancy-looking places have poor food. One can eat modestly but well on $10/day without much difficulty.

Visitors trying to maintain a low-fat diet will not get much help from the locals, who like things greasy. The use of animal fat for frying has mostly died out, with hydrogenated vegetable oil taking its place. It's also taken the same word, so if your dictionary translates *manteca* as lard don't panic. The distinctive Caribbean cooking unfortunately relies heavily on cholesterol-laden coconut oil.

Money

The Costa Rican currency is the Colon, lately quite stable at about 155 to the U.S. Dollar, though with creeping devaluation. Inflation of 10-15% per year in Colon prices has only been partly made up by the devaluations, so Dollar prices are increasing. Hotel prices especially have been inflating rapidly.

Wait to change your Dollars until you arrive. Currencies other than U.S. Dollars are a problem though Canadian Dollars can be changed. Due to recent liberalization of exchange rules life is much easier for the tourist, though lines in the banks can still be horrific. Most better hotels will change money for guests. Don't change on the street, as exchange reform has snuffed out the black market and the money changers that remain are mostly scam artists.

Traveler's checks are the best way to bring money if you can get them free, otherwise cash advances on a VISA card are relatively easy to obtain (2% commission) at branches of the Banco Nacional or Banco Credito Agricola de Cartago. Leftover Colones can be changed back to hard currency without restriction.

Safety

Aside from some specific areas that will be mentioned in the text, your personal safety is not really a concern anywhere in Costa Rica. (Property is another matter.) People in the countryside are almost never a problem unless you're trespassing. In the city, beware of most of the downtown and especially the "Coca-Cola" area where unfortunately many of the long-distance bus stations are.

Remember, even if you don't consider yourself rich, many Costa Ricans can and do live for a year on what you'll spend on this trip. This makes you a target for any pick-pocket or snatch-and-run artist who sees you. Don't help them out by wearing expensive jewelry or watches, and if you must carry the camcorder around town keep a firm grip on it. Wallets are generally safer in a front pocket.

Other than *Homo sapiens*, insects are probably the most serious concern for the birder. Get used to looking for wasps, bees, or especially ants before you put your hands or feet anywhere. The sting of the large *bala* ants in the Caribbean lowlands is reputed to be especially painful. Africanized honeybees are another problem, so keep an eye out for swarms of bees, especially in Guanacaste. If you come upon a nest or swarm, sneak away quietly.

Snakes are much overrated as a threat in the tropical forest; in about 120 days of fieldwork in Costa Rica I have seen only three poisonous snakes and have yet to encounter the much-feared *terciopelo* or fer d'lance. Most such snakes are nocturnal and unlikely to be encountered while birding. If you stay on the trails and watch where you're walking there is no need to worry.

The Ticos

Costa Ricans are very friendly, and can usually be counted on to do their best to help you out. They are genuinely fond of North Americans and other foreigners.

Unfortunately, Ticos are not too good at giving directions, though at least you probably won't be purposely sent in the wrong direction as happens in some countries. Most Costa Ricans live their whole lives in a small area, and cannot relate to the type of directions someone unfamiliar with the local landmarks will need to find something. San José has a perfectly logical grid system of streets and avenues, but virtually no one uses it, instead saying "X meters in such-and-such direction, then X meters in another" from some well-known building, park or other landmark. Maps do no good in this situation. Usually *cien metros* (100 meters) means a city block regardless of the actual distance, but sometimes you will run into someone who is talking about the physical distance. Often you can simply ask *a* (to) your destination and try to get them to point. If they point one way and say another (*izqierda/derecha/ directo* for left/right/straight) go with the finger.

Language

Spanish is the only language of the vast majority of the population, and outside of the better tourist facilities don't expect anyone to speak English. The minor exception is the Caribbean coast where some of the locals speak a Creole English. Menus are often bilingual but watch that the prices are the same on both versions.

Before you leave, work on some phrases you can use when you get lost—you doubtless will despite my best efforts.

Health

Costa Rica is one of the healthiest countries in Latin America due to its relatively advanced standard of living and social spending. Emergency care is free for everyone in Costa Rica, foreigners included. Your principle health risk will be a traffic accident.

Traveler's diarrhea is almost inevitable; bring Pepto-Bismol and Immodium. You might avoid this malady by not drinking any water (don't forget ice) while in the lowlands and eating only hot food that you can see being prepared. On any trip of more than a week you will certainly be exposed to the foreign strains of *E. coli* that cause most problems, so you might as well resign yourself to it.

No area in this book has more than a minuscule risk of malaria so don't let anyone suggest you should take prophylactic medication, as it can have side effects. A more serious problem in 1994 was a Dengue fever outbreak in the Puntarenas area, with a few cases in the Central Valley. The best measure against this disease is to avoid being bitten by nocturnal mosquitoes.

The National Parks

Many of the spots in this book are protected and kept public within Costa Rica's fine system of national parks. Technically no park or reserve is open to the public before 8 a.m. but in many cases one can sneak in or just amble by and pay your entrance later. The administrators generally realize that such a late hour is not acceptable to many tourists but the bureaucratic, centralized system is slow to change.

As of early 1994 the entrance fee was 200 Colones or about $1.30, up from 25 Colones five years ago. The central parks administration would like to charge foreigners more but at present is prohibited by law from discriminating by nationality. If they succeed in getting the law changed expect the entrance to go to at least 500 Colones. After all, they say, it costs $25 to get into the Epcot Center so you shouldn't mind shelling out.

Perhaps some of that money will go to improve the generally poor information, maps, etc. that are available. Check at each station to see what is available.

Resources

The main source for birders is Stiles and Skutch's *Birds of Costa Rica*, with Ridgely's *Birds of Panama* second. Stiles and Skutch is a difficult book to learn to use due to the vast quantity of information that must be waded through to reach what you want. It is also a bit heavy to use in the field, so it might be worth getting the plates bound separately. Ridgely is better for beginner's identification problems because he discusses similar species under each account, but descriptions of voices are better in the Costa Rican book. The quality of the artwork is similar in both books.

The second edition of Ridgely has accounts and illustrations for all the species found in Costa Rica but not in Panama, but these are in the back and there is no specific Costa Rican locality information for birds found in both countries. Behavior and habitat information are much better in Stiles and Skutch. In other words, bring both books. A Mexican book might be useful as well, especially in Guanacaste, but is not really necessary like it was in the old days.

You will need a map, of which several are available. None is particularly accurate when it comes to detail. The best and probably most widely available in North America is the International Travel Map Productions *Traveler's Map of Costa Rica*.

For general tourist information, the Lonely Planet *Costa Rica: a travel survival kit* and *The New Key to Costa Rica* are generally the best choices. *Costa Rica: A Natural Destination* has some information for birders but also has considerable fluff.

The ICT tourist office under the Plaza de la Cultura in downtown San José is very helpful with specific questions.

How to use this book

Each site in this book merits at least a morning's birding (usually much more) so each stands independent. The book is not organized in any particular fashion (i.e. the "loop routes" unfortunately popularized by the late Jim Lane) to help you plan your trip, though see the suggested itineraries in the back. Get a map and study the birdlists to decide where you want to put your energies.

The lists are not intended to be comprehensive, as for some areas like La Selva or Braulio Carrillo that would involve 400 species. They are meant as a study guide for the first-time visitor, to be looked over the night before in preparation for the common birds of the area. Many of the commonest birds are not mentioned, especially if they are large and conspicuous. Do your homework, as obviously the less time you spend with your face in the book the more birds you'll see.

Some specialties that you don't want to miss if you get a shot are also mentioned, even if they're scarce. Don't use the lists as a reference to what is possible in an area, see the distribution section of Stiles and Skutch. It's up to you to sort out which species are present if you come during the Northern summer and which are not.

Names on the lists closely follow that book with some exceptions: *Turdus* are all called "thrush" rather than "robin." *Myioborus* "redstarts" are called "whitestart," and "Mistletoe" Tyrannulet is called Paltry Tyrannulet as in most other sources. The Atlantic race of the Plain Wren is referred to as Canebrake Wren though they are presently lumped.

San José

Getting around San José will be the first and perhaps most memorable adventure of your trip. Costa Rica's capital doesn't yet have the smog of Mexico City, the bad drivers of Guatemala, or the gridlock of San Salvador, but with the present rate of economic growth and vehicle importation it may catch up soon. Be prepared to get lost and keep your humor as much as possible.

A few notes about driving in San José: generally keep an eye on the front of your car and let other drivers worry about the behind. Most signs are of the international type with the possible (and important) exception of "No hay paso" which means you are entering a one-way street the wrong way. Usually oncoming traffic will emphasize this for you.

Stop signs are treated liberally by the natives, and the locals even run red lights in front of the traffic police. If you try this you might be hit up for a bribe. Where there is a stop sign and a traffic light at the same intersection the light has priority. Especially on the highway east-bound towards Cartago there are places where there are two lights: one controls left turns and the other is for through traffic.

The traffic circles on some San José byways can be difficult to get the hang of if you don't have them at home, but the general rule is to enter in the left lane if you are going through or left and in the right lane for the short right turn. Then yield to anyone in the circle before taking your place in the controlled chaos.

Generally the birder will want to stay at a hotel on the edge of town, such as the Hotel Irazú. This hotel is often part of discount air and hotel packages. It is also an important landmark in the following discussion of how to cross the city.

If you are leaving early enough in the morning it will not matter much which route you use, though navigating without enough light to read the few street signs can be a problem. Generally, when traffic is light the downtown route would be better due to its simplicity. When daytime traffic sets in the northern route through the lovely industrial suburb of La Uruca is superior.

City Route:

Technically the Pan-American highway passes right through the center of San José, and some signs direct you that way. If coming from the airport and heading towards Cartago you basically want to continue on the freeway past the Irazú and Corobicí hotels, and then take a left at a light just past an Exxon station and opposite a large park. Much of the traffic will go this way so it will be more obvious than the one small "San José" sign might make it seem. This will put you on the Paseo Colon, which is actually Avenida Central (0). Continue and jog right with most traffic onto Avenida 2 as you enter the downtown— continue straight about 5 km to the suburb of San Pedro where you will see a traffic circle with some fountains in the middle. Go around the traffic circle and straight to the suburb of Curridabat. After another 4 km you will go over the freeway to Cartago. Be sure to get in the middle lane (marked "Tres Ríos/Cartago") or you're in trouble. Merge as soon as possible at the beginning of what appears to be a long merge lane but is not. Shortly after you will need to pay a toll (one way only), 40 Colons in 1994.

Westbound on the same freeway, watch for the traffic cops on the long downhill before the toll booths. Don't take the freeway to its end but take an exit for San Pedro and return to the fountains mentioned above. As you continue towards the city you will be eventually confronted with a "No Hay Paso" sign and be forced right. Take the first left and continue towards the downtown on Avenida 1. On through downtown either jog left on Calle 20 or right on Calle 22 and continue westward until you hit the freeway.

Northern route:

To avoid the downtown traffic when coming from the airport look for some strange signs which show the convoluted route to the Irazú hotel. After seeing these and a large hospital ("CCSS") on the right, you pass under a pedestrian overpass and then exit right before the freeway goes over an overpass. On the traffic circle below, go nearly all the way around until you are almost going back the way you came and exit, getting in the right lane. After a few blocks you will see the large LACSA administration building on the left and will want to turn right at a major intersection. This will take you through La Uruca, where most of the heavy equipment etc. dealers in Costa Rica are. After about 3 km there is a fork with a Shell station in the middle: take the left. This continues straight except for one detour until you reach an intersection with a sign for "Circunvalacion Sur" and bear right. After two traffic circles that you cross and go straight you will need to exit right at a large shopping center, just after Taco Bell, to get to the San Pedro traffic circle. After going around the circle and left you will be on the highway to Curridabat as in the other eastbound directions.

Westbound this route is far superior. At the San Pedro circle, go right onto the beltway and through the first two circles. At a T intersection you will need to make a left, then continue straight for about 5 km to the fork with the Shell station, where you merge to the right. At the intersection by the LACSA building, you can then go straight to the freeway and airport, left to the Hotel Irazú, or right to Heredia for Volcán Poás, Virgen del Socorro, etc.

It would seem that the route just described would also be the way to get on the Guápiles highway for Braulio Carrillo National Park, Finca La Selva, or Limón, but there are no ramps where it crosses the freeway. Coming from the airport, it is probably easiest to work your way into the downtown grid and get on Calle 3 northbound, which will eventually turn into the Guápiles highway. From Cartago, bear right at the San Pedro circle and through the next one to the Guadelupe circle just after the Lubriquick and a large cemetery. Go around the circle and left. At the fifth traffic light by a La Republica (newspaper) building turn right onto the highway.

Cartago:

Costa Rica's old capital doesn't present nearly as much of a challenge to the visitor. For Paraíso (Tapantí National Park) and Turrialba stay on the freeway down off the continental divide at Ochomogo until two lanes curve off to the left and one goes straight to Cerro de la Muerte and the Zona Sur. After a large cemetery as you enter town, take a right at the first opportunity. After two blocks take a left and follow that street all the way through town to Paraíso.

Westbound it is a different set of streets but the same idea. The route is fairly well-signed for San José.

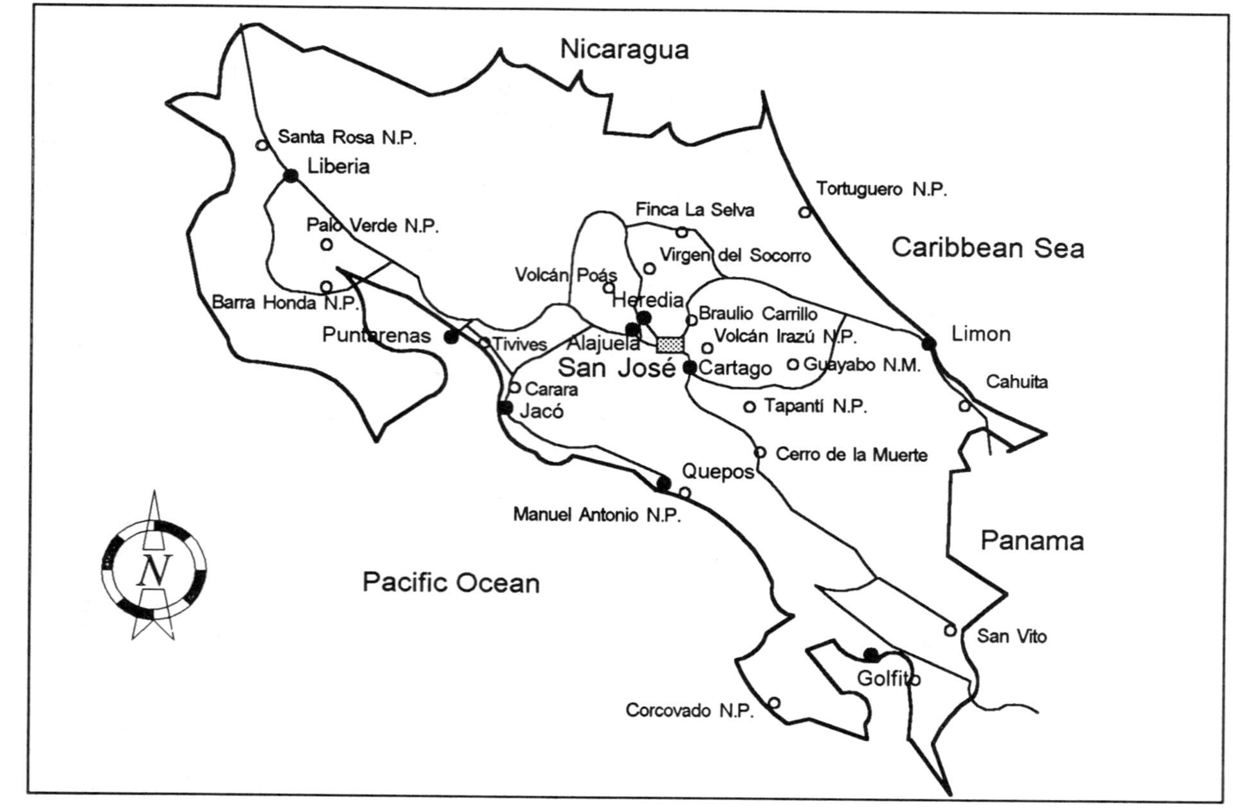
Nicaragua
Santa Rosa N.P.
Liberia
Tortuguero N.P.
Finca La Selva
Palo Verde N.P.
Virgen del Socorro
Caribbean Sea
Volcán Poás
Heredia
Barra Honda N.P.
Braulio Carrillo
Puntarenas
Tivives
Alajuela
Volcán Irazú N.P.
Limon
San José
Cartago
Guayabo N.M.
Carara
Cahuita
Jacó
Tapantí N.P.
Cerro de la Muerte
Quepos
Manuel Antonio N.P.
N
Panama
Pacific Ocean
San Vito
Golfito
Corcovado N.P.

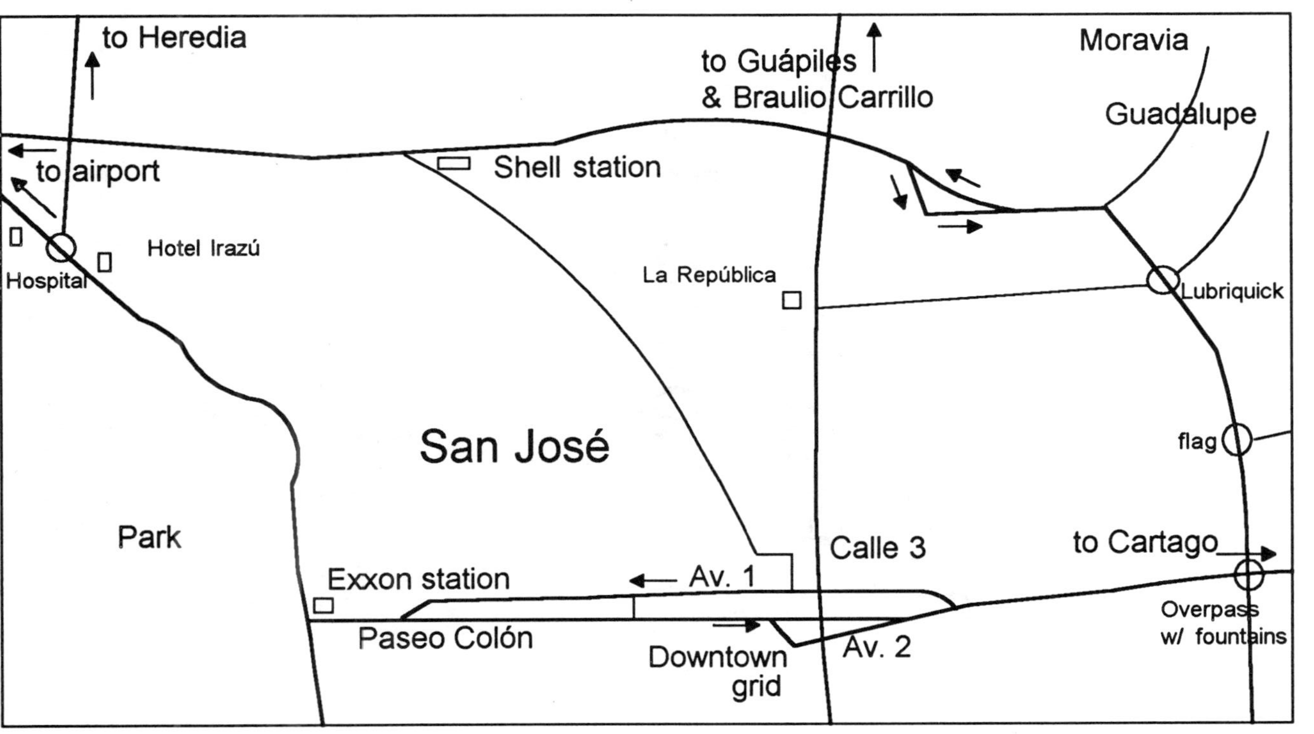
to Heredia
to Guápiles
& Braulio Carrillo
Moravia
Guadalupe
to airport
Shell station
Hotel Irazú
Hospital
La República
Lubriquick
San José
flag
Park
Calle 3
to Cartago
Exxon station
Av. 1
Paseo Colón
Downtown
grid
Av. 2
Overpass
w/ fountains

The Pacific Lowlands

The Pacific Lowlands

The narrow band of moist lowland forest from Carara southeast to the Panamanian border contains some of the best birding in Costa Rica. Unfortunately the areas of undamaged forest are getting smaller and more difficult to reach. A number of endemics make this zone essential for the visiting birder.

This area also has some of Costa Rica's nicest beaches as a diversion. This has both good and bad effects as the accessibility from San José means big crowds on weekends, so schedule accordingly. Accommodation is well-placed and plentiful as a result of the demand, though prices can be high in the "summer" season and Easter weekend is out of the question. Good value can be had in the off-season, however, especially in Jacó.

Carara Biological Reserve

This reserve, while not a national park per se, provides the easiest access to good Pacific lowland forest. A reasonably large population of Scarlet Macaws is the principal attraction, but a wide variety of other species can be seen. The best area can be overrun with tourists so arrive early.

The accessible forest is right on the coastal highway near the beach town of Jacó, about two hours from San José. Take an exit from the freeway about 11 km beyond the airport towards San Ramon and pass through Atenas and Orotina. About 300 meters beyond the Río Tárcoles bridge is a road off to the left into the forest. This is the main birding area. This area has suffered many car break-ins, so if there are no tour bus drivers around to watch your car you should leave it at the restaurant on the other side of the bridge and walk (good birding anyway) to the entrance.

There are also some short trails through nice forest at the headquarters about 3 km along the road toward Jacó. Here you can pay your entrance fee as well.

Many tourists visit this area as a day trip from San José but you would need a very early start to make this worthwhile for birding. You'll need to get well down the trail before the dudes show up. There is lots of accommodation at Jacó and a few cabinas and one lodge in Tárcoles/ Playa Azul.

The Scarlet Macaws can be seen easily early or late in the day as they fly between the reserve and roosting areas to the northwest. During the day you might get a look at a pair feeding somewhere in the reserve.

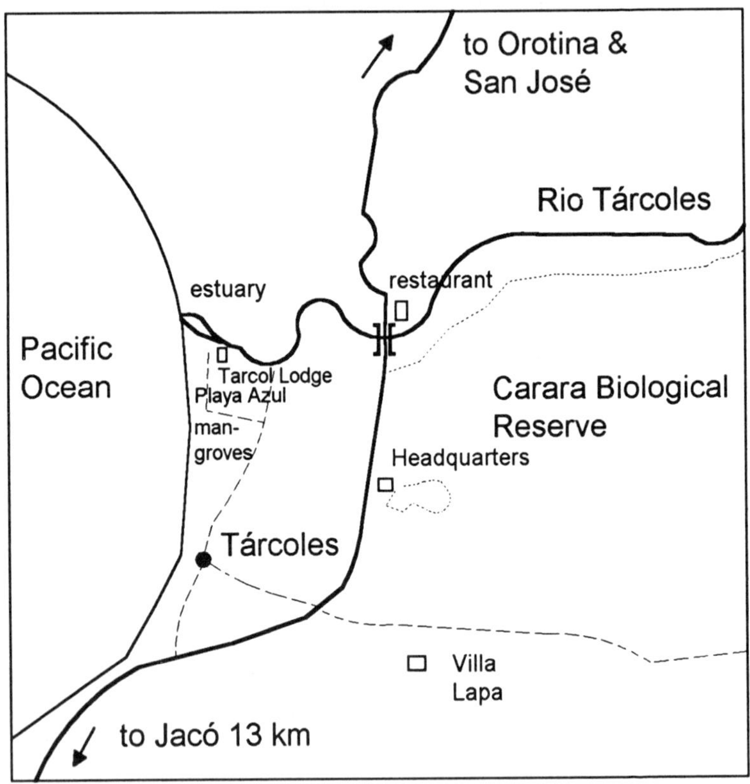

Birds of Carara Biological Reserve

Great Tinamou
Gray Hawk
Broad-winged Hawk
Crested Caracara
Yellow-headed Caracara
Crested Guan
White-throated Crake
Short-billed Pigeon
Inca Dove
Blue Ground-Dove
White-tipped Dove
Gray-chested Dove
Crimson-fronted Parakeet
Scarlet Macaw
Orange-chinned Parakeet
White-crowned Parrot
Red-lored Parrot
Mealy Parrot
Yellow-naped Parrot
Squirrel Cuckoo
Lesser Nighthawk
Band-rumped Swift
Bronzy Hermit
Band-tailed Barbthroat
Long-tailed Hermit
Little Hermit
Scaly-breasted Hummingbird
Crowned Woodnymph
Blue-throated Goldentail
Rufous-tailed Hummingbird
Purple-crowned Fairy
Long-billed Starthroat
Black-headed Trogon
Baird's Trogon
Violaceous Trogon
Slaty-tailed Trogon
White-whiskered Puffbird
Rufous-tailed Jacamar
Fiery-billed Aracari
Golden-naped Woodpecker
Lineated Woodpecker
Pale-billed Woodpecker
Buff-throated Foliage-gleaner
Plain Xenops
Tawny-winged Woodcreeper
Wedge-billed Woodcreeper
Barred Woodcreeper
Buff-throated Woodcreeper
Streak-headed Woodcreeper
Great Antshrike
Barred Antshrike
Black-hooded Antshrike
Dot-winged Antwren
Chestnut-backed Antbird
Black-faced Antthrush
Spectacled Antpitta
S. Beardless Tyrannulet
Ochre-bellied Flycatcher

Northern Bentbill
Eye-ringed Flatbill
Golden-crowned Spadebill
Ruddy-tailed Flycatcher
Yellow-bellied Flycatcher
Rufous Mourner
White-winged Becard
Yellow-billed Cotinga
Thrushlike Manakin
Blue-crowned Manakin
Gray-breasted Martin
Black-bellied Wren
Rufous-breasted Wren
House Wren
Tropical Gnatcatcher
Yellow-green Vireo
Tennessee Warbler
Bananaquit
Scarlet-thighed Dacnis
Green Honeycreeper
Yellow-crowned Euphonia
Red-crowned Ant-Tanager
Buff-throated Saltator
Orange-billed Sparrow
Blue-black Grassquit
White-collared Seedeater
Yellow-billed Cacique

Common Tody-Flycatcher
Yellow-olive Flycatcher
Royal Flycatcher
Black-tailed Flycatcher
Bright-rumped Attila
Dusky-capped Flycatcher
Rufous Piha
Three-wattled Bellbird
Orange-collared Manakin
Red-capped Manakin
Mangrove Swallow
Riverside Wren
Plain Wren
Long-billed Gnatwren
Yellow-throated Vireo
Lesser Greenlet
Chestnut-sided Warbler
Golden-hooded Tanager
Blue Dacnis
Red-legged Honeycreeper
Thick-billed Euphonia
Summer Tanager
Blue-black Grosbeak
Black-striped Sparrow
Variable Seedeater
Northern Oriole
Scarlet-rumped Cacique

Río Tárcoles Estuary

While unlikely to produce many species not found in North America, this is the most convenient spot to pad your list with terns, herons, and a few migrant shorebirds. Mid tide is best if you can figure out when that is.

To reach the best area for viewing, take the first right after the Carara reserve headquarters, clearly marked for Tárcoles. At a T intersection in town go right back to the north and continue about 3 km to Playa Azul. Bear right to avoid the beach until you reach the Tarcol Lodge (tremendously overpriced at $88 per/person with food but convenient).

The sandbar at the mouth of the river usually has a flock of gulls, terns, pelicans, and Black Skimmers, and the whole area can be good for shorebirds and herons depending on the tide. Boat-billed Herons roost along the river upstream and can be seen from a good vantage point such as the one near "Crocodile Jungle Tours" dock.

A patch of mangroves on the road in to Playa Azul might produce herons, Mangrove Black-Hawk, Mangrove Hummingbird, Tropical Pewee, Scrub Greenlet, Rufous-browed Peppershrike, or other mangrove specialties.

Birds of the Río Tárcoles Estuary

Magnificent Frigatebird
Royal Tern
Laughing Gull
Brown Pelican
Roseate Spoonbill
White Ibis
Boat-billed Heron
Tricolored Heron
Sandwich Tern
Elegant Tern
Black Skimmer
Neotropic Cormorant
Wood Stork
Yellow-crowned Night-Heron
Great Blue Heron
Little Blue Heron

Snowy Egret	Great Egret
Black-bellied Plover	Willet
Whimbrel	Black-necked Stilt
Ruddy Turnstone	Spotted Sandpiper
Semipalmated Sandpiper	Western Sandpiper
Least Sandpiper	

Tivives Mangroves

At the small beach town of Tivives there is access to good mangroves. Unlike most of the mangrove areas in the country a boat is not necessary.

The road to Tivives is well-marked off the highway between Carara and Caldera, the port near Puntarenas. Proceed down the gravel road watching for a side road with a blue metal gate on the left. If you reach a somewhat inexplicable police checkpoint you've gone too far, though there is a small estuary with a few shorebirds on the far (south) end of town. At the end of the side road, climb the fence and walk back into the woods which will eventually, depending on water levels, be too muddy to walk. In the dry season rubber boots are not really necessary. Here Mangrove Warbler is common and other mangrove specialties including Mangrove Vireo are possible.

Manuel Antonio National Park

This park is famous for its beautiful beaches and is very popular with Costa Rica's youth. There is some good habitat too but it is not necessarily worth the high prices and commotion. The road out to Manuel Antonio from the grungy port town of Quepos is now lined with tourist development, and keep in mind if you want to swim that there is no sewage treatment facility for any of those hotels.

Quepos is best reached by the highway that continues beyond Jacó through miles of oil palm plantations. The pavement is in bad condition most of the way, and turns to good gravel for about the last 20 km. Quepos is about 3 hours from San José. There is lots of accommodation in all price ranges in Quepos and Manuel Antonio.

Due to crowd control measures it is a bit hard to get into the park before 8 a.m. though there is a back road with a gate. Park rangers here are the least friendly anywhere in the system. There is birding along the road to Quepos for species of broken habitats and second growth, but the best habitat is on Punta Catedral and past the first beaches.

There is also a patch of scrubby mangroves north of Quepos that can produce Mangrove Hummingbird and other specialties if you are lucky.

Birds of Manuel Antonio National Park and vicinity

Brown Booby	Roadside Hawk
Broad-winged Hawk	Yellow-headed Caracara
Gray-headed Chachalaca	Gray-necked Wood-Rail
Laughing Gull	Royal Tern
Sandwich Tern	Elegant Tern
Pale-vented Pigeon	Scaled Pigeon
Blue Ground-Dove	White-tipped Dove
Orange-chinned Parakeet	White-crowned Parrot
Red-lored Parrot	Smooth-billed Ani
Ferruginous Pygmy-Owl	Pauraque
Vaux's Swift	Lesser Swallow-tailed Swift
Little Hermit	Blue-throated Goldentail
Charming Hummingbird	Rufous-tailed Hummingbird
Purple-crowned Fairy	Ruby-throated Hummingbird
Ringed Kingfisher	Green Kingfisher

Golden-naped Woodpecker
Tawny-winged Woodcreeper
Black-hooded Antshrike
Chestnut-backed Antbird
Yellow-olive Flycatcher
Great Crested Flycatcher
White-winged Becard
Golden-collared Manakin
Gray-breasted Martin
Black-bellied Wren
Plain Wren
Tropical Gnatcatcher
Lesser Greenlet
Prothonotary Warbler
Worm-eating Warbler
Bananaquit
Shining Honeycreeper
Yellow-crowned Euphonia
Buff-throated Saltator
Orange-billed Sparrow
White-collared Seedeater
Eastern Meadowlark
House Sparrow

Red-crowned Woodpecker
Streak-headed Woodcreeper
Dot-winged Antwren
S. Beardless Tyrannulet
Yellow-bellied Flycatcher
Streaked Flycatcher
Black-crowned Tityra
Red-capped Manakin
S. Rough-winged Swallow
Riverside Wren
Long-billed Gnatwren
Philadelphia Vireo
Tennessee Warbler
Chestnut-sided Warbler
Kentucky Warbler
Golden-hooded Tanager
Red-legged Honeycreeper
Summer Tanager
Blue-black Grosbeak
Black-striped Sparrow
Variable Seedeater
Northern Oriole

Corcovado National Park

Corcovado National Park is something of an enigma as it has some of the best habitat in the country and some of the worst access. Ongoing problems with gold miners resulted in the park being temporarily closed to tourists in March 1994. This has happened several times in the past so inquire locally before planning your trip.

Access is difficult, and you are better off not having a car to worry about while you are in the park. Fly-in tours are one possibility. Despite (or because of) all this, birding can be spectacular with large flocks of Scarlet Macaws, a good chance for Great Curassow, and even the possibility of Baird's Tapir or Jaguar.

The easiest access is to fly into the airstrip at Sirena from Golfito or San José. This is of course expensive. Inquire at any travel agency in San José for prices and options.

There are several options to hike in, all requiring at least six hours of walking in the heat. The best choice is probably to take a taxi from the town of Puerto Jimenez around the end of the peninsula to the mining town of Carate and walk up the beach a little over 3 km to the La Leona station. From here you can get an early start to walk the beach. Low tide is a must as some areas are headlands with inadequate trails above. If you make it past all the river crossings and are used to the heat, this can be done in six or seven hours. For more details on walking options, see Joseph Franke's book *Costa Rica's National Parks and Reserves*.

Camping in the chigger-infested clearing at the Sirena station is your most reliable option, though there is some possibility of accommodation in the park building and/or meals if you can arrange it ahead of time with the National Parks office in San José or the local park office in Puerto Jimenez. Be sure radio contact is made to confirm your arrival or it may come as a surprise to the station you plan to visit.

Sirena has the best facilities though the forest is not as good being mostly second-growth. Some of the best birds don't seem to mind, however, so the area close to the station can be excellent. The San Pedrillo area in the north has the best forest; it is perhaps best visited from one of the lodges on the north side of the park such as Marenco Biological Station or Drake Bay Wilderness Camp.

Birds of Corcovado National Park

Great Tinamou
Little Tinamou
Brown Booby
King Vulture
White Hawk
Mangrove Black-Hawk
Red-throated Caracara
Laughing Falcon
Bat Falcon
Crested Guan
Great Curassow
Marbled Wood-Quail
White-throated Crake
Gray-necked Wood-Rail
Sungrebe
Wilson's Plover
Surfbird
Sanderling
Least Sandpiper
Laughing Gull
Pale-vented Pigeon
Short-billed Pigeon
White-tipped Dove
Gray-chested Dove
Ruddy Quail-Dove
Crimson-fronted Parakeet
Scarlet Macaw
Orange-chinned Parakeet
Brown-hooded Parrot
White-crowned Parrot
Mealy Parrot
Squirrel Cuckoo
Striped Cuckoo
Smooth-billed Ani
Spectacled Owl
Mottled Owl
Pauraque
Band-rumped Swift
L. Swallow-tailed Swift
Bronzy Hermit
Band-tailed Barbthroat
Long-tailed Hermit
Little Hermit
Scaly-breasted Hummingbird
White-necked Jacobin
Violet-headed Hummingbird
White-crested Coquette
Garden Emerald
Crowned Woodnymph
Blue-throated Goldentail
Charming Hummingbird
Mangrove Hummingbird
Rufous-tailed Hummingbird
Purple-crowned Fairy
Long-billed Starthroat
Baird's Trogon
Violaceous Trogon
Black-throated Trogon

Slaty-tailed Trogon
Ringed Kingfisher
White-necked Puffbird
Rufous-tailed Jacamar
Chestnut-mandibled Toucan
Golden-naped Woodpecker
Pale-billed Woodpecker
Striped Foliage-gleaner
Scaly-throated Leaftosser
Long-tailed Woodcreeper
Buff-throated Woodcreeper
Streak-headed Woodcreeper
Black-hooded Antshrike
Slaty Antwren
Dusky Antbird
Chestnut-backed Antbird
Black-faced Antthrush
Paltry Tyrannulet
S. Beardless Tyrannulet
Yellow Tyrannulet
Northern Bentbill
Golden-crowned Spadebill
Sulphur-rumped Flycatcher
Rufous Mourner
Cinnamon Becard
Rufous Piha
Yellow-billed Cotinga
Golden-collared Manakin
Red-capped Manakin
Riverside Wren
White-breasted Wood-Wren
Long-billed Gnatwren

Blue-crowned Motmot
Am. Pygmy Kingfisher
White-whiskered Puffbird
Fiery-billed Aracari
Olivaceous Piculet
Red-crowned Woodpecker
Slaty Spinetail
Plain Xenops
Tawny-winged Woodcreeper
Wedge-billed Woodcreeper
Black-striped Woodcreeper
Great Antshrike
Plain Antvireo
Dot-winged Antwren
Bare-crowned Antbird
Bicolored Antbird
Spectacled Antpitta
Yellow-bellied Tyrannulet
Ochre-bellied Flycatcher
Scale-crested Pygmy-Tyrant
Eye-ringed Flatbill
Ruddy-tailed Flycatcher
Bright-rumped Attila
Dusky-capped Flycatcher
White-winged Becard
Turquoise Cotinga
Thrushlike Manakin
Blue-crowned Manakin
Black-bellied Wren
Plain Wren
S. Nightingale-Wren
Tropical Gnatcatcher

Scrub Greenlet
Tawny-crowned Greenlet
Lesser Greenlet
Green Shrike-Vireo
Tennessee Warbler
Prothonotary Warbler
Kentucky Warbler
Mourning Warbler
Gray-crowned Yellowthroat
Canada Warbler
Buff-rumped Warbler
Bananaquit
Golden-hooded Tanager
Scarlet-thighed Dacnis
Blue Dacnis
Shining Honeycreeper
Red-legged Honeycreeper
Yellow-crowned Euphonia
White-vented Euphonia
Olive-backed Euphonia
Gray-headed Tanager
White-throated Shrike-Tanager
White-shouldered Tanager
Black-cheeked Ant-Tanager
Hepatic Tanager
Summer Tanager
Buff-throated Saltator
Blue-black Grosbeak
Orange-billed Sparrow
Black-striped Sparrow
Blue-black Grassquit
Variable Seedeater
Yellow-bellied Seedeater
Thick-billed Seed-Finch
Northern Oriole
Yellow-billed Cacique
Scarlet-rumped Cacique

Golfito National Wildlife Refuge

Some forest in the hills above the town of Golfito exists as an inferior alternative to birding Corcovado. The habitat is good but on steep ground so birding is restricted to the road.

The road up to some communications towers starts by the first soccer field on the right as you come into town, and passes by the Bar Deportivo. It is steep but should be passible in any season with a 2WD vehicle. Once the road finally levels off the habitat becomes mostly second-growth or active fields. The birdlist here would be like a thin version of Corcovado's.

Guanacaste

Guanacaste

Costa Rica's northwestern province of Guanacaste provides easy access to the dry forest typical of western Mexico and the Pacific slope of Central America. Most of the area is deforested and full of exotic African savannah grasses but various parks preserve patches of remanent or second-growth forest.

The Tropical Dry Forest has the most pronounced dry season of the various Costa Rican life zones, and many trees drop their leaves during the driest period from December through March. Nonetheless, some of these same trees are flowering and birding is generally good. The weather can be a problem, as the wind fairly howls down off Lake Nicaragua and can severely reduce productivity not much after 9 a.m. The National Parks don't officially open until 8 a.m. so camping makes good sense if you can bring the needed minimum of equipment.

Birding is relatively easy due to the sparse vegetation and open country, and you can find most of the specialties in a short time. There are a number of nice parks in Guanacaste that are not included here because they are difficult to access or do not have substantially different birdlife. Of considerable importance from a conservation standpoint are Guanacaste National Park across the road from Santa Rosa and Rincón de la Vieja National Park above Liberia. These are well worth a visit if you have time.

The Lomas de Barbudal Biological Reserve mentioned in some guidebooks burned in almost its entirety in March 1994. It unfortunately won't be much of a birding site for years to come, if ever.

Much of Costa Rica's mass tourism development is taking place in Guanacaste near the Nicaraguan border, which may eventually make access more affordable as flights go to the recently-upgraded airport at Liberia. Until then, there is accommodation near the beaches at Playa Hermosa, Playas del Coco, Tamarindo, Sámara, and in the larger towns of the province.

The Hacienda La Pacífica resort complex, which has decent habitat right on the grounds and along the nearby river, is popular with birders. Boat-billed Herons roost along the river. The complex is about 5 km north of Cañas, within easy reach of Santa Rosa and Palo Verde National Parks. Double rooms are about $70 in the high season.

Santa Rosa National Park

This park preserves some history from Costa Rica's less than bellicose past as well as some excellent tropical dry forest. If the road to Playa Naranjo is open and passible, the best birding is down near the beaches and around Estero Real. If not, there is plenty of good habitat accessible by paved road.

Santa Rosa park has been expanded in recent years in an attempt to rehabilitate some of the unproductive cattle country on every side, and

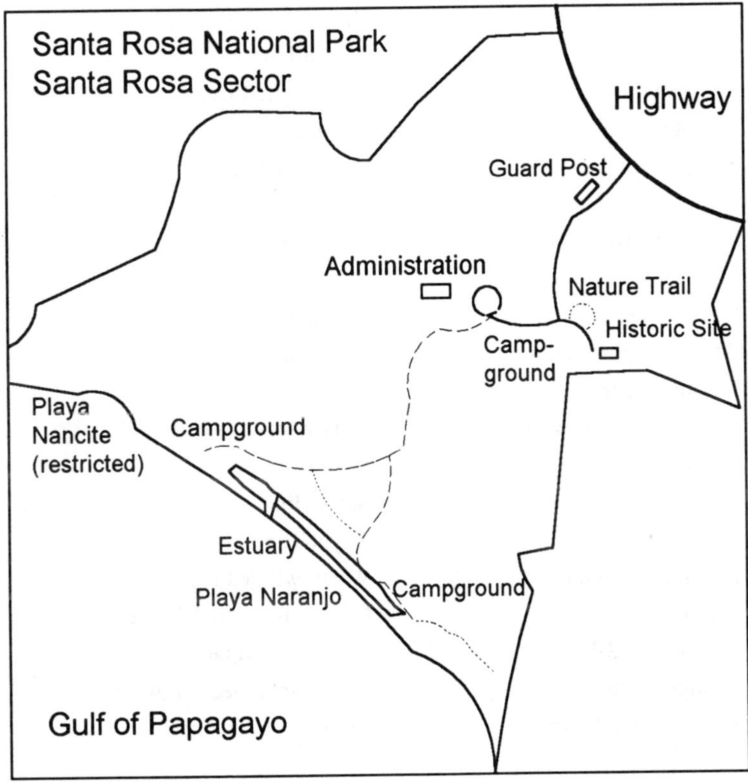

has been made part of the Guanacaste Conservation Area in some sort of bureaucratic reshuffling. The best birding is still in the Santa Rosa sector itself.

The park is easily reached from Liberia, 35 km along the Pan-American highway towards Nicaragua. There are plenty of accommodations in Liberia. At a pleasant campground near the park headquarters, you can listen to Pacific Screech-Owls instead of traffic and barking dogs. There are also campgrounds at Playa Naranjo, but these can be occupied by noisy surfers when the road is open and require a 14 km walk during the rainy season.

Birds of Santa Rosa National Park

Thicket Tinamou
Brown Booby
Brown Pelican
Magnificent Frigatebird
King Vulture
White-tailed Kite
Double-toothed Kite
Plumbeous Kite
Mangrove Black-Hawk
Great Black-Hawk
White-tailed Hawk
Zone-tailed Hawk
Harris' Hawk
Roadside Hawk
Gray Hawk
Osprey
Crested Caracara
Laughing Falcon
American Kestrel
Plain Chachalaca
Crested Guan
Great Curassow
Spot-bellied Bobwhite
Gray-necked Wood-Rail
Black-bellied Plover
Willet
Whimbrel
Sanderling
Laughing Gull
Royal Tern
Red-billed Pigeon
White-winged Dove
Inca Dove
Common Ground-Dove
Blue Ground-Dove
White-tipped Dove
Orange-fronted Parakeet
Orange-chinned Parakeet
White-fronted Parrot
Yellow-naped Parrot

Mangrove Cuckoo
Squirrel Cuckoo
Barn Owl
Ferruginous Pygmy-Owl
Lesser Nighthawk
Green-breasted Mango
Blue-throated Goldentail
Steely-vented Hummingbird
Plain-capped Starthroat
Black-headed Trogon
Violaceous Trogon
Blue-crowned Motmot
Collared Aracari
Hoffman's Woodpecker
Pale-billed Woodpecker
Ivory-billed Woodcreeper
Barred Antshrike
Northern Bentbill
Greenish Elaenia
Yellow-olive Flycatcher
Bright-rumped Attila
Nutting's Flycatcher
Brown-crested Flycatcher
Boat-billed Flycatcher
Streaked Flycatcher
Piratic Flycatcher
Western Kingbird
Rose-throated Becard
Black-crowned Tityra
Gray-breasted Martin
Barn Swallow
Rufous-naped Wren
Banded Wren

Lesser Ground-Cuckoo
Groove-billed Ani
Pacific Screech-Owl
Mottled Owl
Pauraque
Fork-tailed Emerald
Cinnamon Hummingbird
Rufous-tailed Hummingbird
Ruby-throated Hummingbird
Elegant Trogon
Turquoise-browed Motmot
White-necked Puffbird
Keel-billed Toucan
Lineated Woodpecker
Ruddy Woodcreeper
Streak-headed Woodcreeper
N. Beardless Tyrannulet
Yellow-bellied Elaenia
Common Tody-Flycatcher
Stub-tailed Spadebill
Dusky-capped Flycatcher
Great Crested Flycatcher
Great Kiskadee
Social Flycatcher
Sulphur-bellied Flycatcher
Tropical Kingbird
Scissor-tailed Flycatcher
Masked Tityra
Long-tailed Manakin
Mangrove Swallow
White-throated Magpie-Jay
Rufous & White Wren
Plain Wren

House Wren
Clay-colored Thrush
Yellow-green Vireo
Tennessee Warbler
Northern Waterthrush
Rufous-capped Warbler
Thick-billed Euphonia
Blue-gray Tanager
Western Tanager
Buff-throated Saltator
Indigo Bunting
White-collared Seedeater
Northern Oriole
Spot-breasted Oriole
White-lored Gnatcatcher
Swainson's Thrush
Lesser Greenlet
Yellow Warbler
Gray-crowned Yellowthroat
Red-legged Honeycreeper
Scrub Euphonia
Summer Tanager
Grayish Saltator
Rose-breasted Grosbeak
Olive Sparrow
Yellow-faced Grassquit
Streak-backed Oriole

Palo Verde National Park

The marshes at the mouth of the Río Tempisque are the main attraction here though they are difficult to access. This is the last stronghold of the Jabiru in Central America, and it can be found with some regularity. There is good Tropical Dry Forest as well, and an impressive number of large iguanas. Africanized bees can be a problem here.

The park is reached by a bad road from the town of Bagaces on the Pan-American highway. The road should be passible year-round. If you get a flat tire return to town and get it fixed before proceeding, as there is little traffic to take you out if you get another. The nearest hotels are in Liberia, and there is camping in the park.

The marshes hold large numbers of water birds in the November to March dry season though some leave as water becomes scarce after January. Mostly the species are the same as in Florida but numbers can be impressive. The best place to view the marshes is between the dock and the OTS station. Otherwise there are a number of trails that lead into the forest.

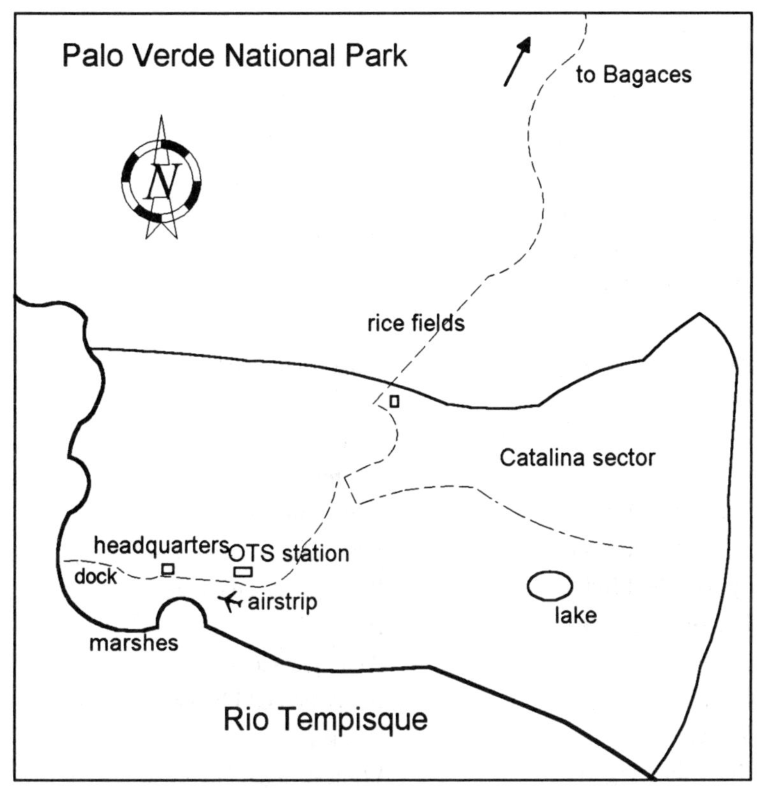

Birds of Palo Verde National Park

Thicket Tinamou
Pied-billed Grebe
Neotropic Cormorant
Great Blue Heron
Snowy Egret
Black-crowned Night-Heron
Boat-billed Heron
Glossy Ibis
Jabiru

Least Grebe
Anhinga
Bare-throated Tiger-Heron
Great Egret
Green Heron
Yellow-crowned Night-Heron
White Ibis
Roseate Spoonbill
Wood Stork

Black-bellied Whistling-Duck
Muscovy
Blue-winged Teal
American Wigeon
L. Yellow-headed Vulture
White-tailed Kite
Double-toothed Kite
Mangrove Black-Hawk
White-tailed Hawk
Harris' Hawk
Gray Hawk
Crested Caracara
American Kestrel
Spot-bellied Bobwhite
Gray-necked Wood-Rail
Common Moorhen
Limpkin
Willet
Red-billed Pigeon
Inca Dove
Blue Ground-Dove
Orange-fronted Parakeet
White-fronted Parrot
Mangrove Cuckoo
Squirrel Cuckoo
Barn Owl
Ferruginous Pygmy-Owl
Lesser Nighthawk
Green-breasted Mango
Cinnamon Hummingbird
Rufous-tailed Hummingbird
Ruby-throated Hummingbird
Elegant Trogon

Fulvous Whistling-Duck
Northern Pintail
Northern Shoveler
Masked Duck
King Vulture
Snail Kite
Plumbeous Kite
Great Black-Hawk
Zone-tailed Hawk
Roadside Hawk
Osprey
Laughing Falcon
Plain Chachalaca
White-throated Crake
Purple Gallinule
American Coot
Black-bellied Plover
Black Tern
White-winged Dove
Common Ground-Dove
White-tipped Dove
Orange-chinned Parakeet
Yellow-naped Parrot
Lesser Ground-Cuckoo
Groove-billed Ani
Pacific Screech-Owl
Mottled Owl
Pauraque
Fork-tailed Emerald
Steely-vented Hummingbird
Plain-capped Starthroat
Black-headed Trogon
Violaceous Trogon

Turquoise-browed Motmot
Keel-billed Toucan
Lineated Woodpecker
Ivory-billed Woodcreeper
Barred Antshrike
Yellow-bellied Elaenia
Common Tody-Flycatcher
Stub-tailed Spadebill
Dusky-capped Flycatcher
Great Crested Flycatcher
Great Kiskadee
Social Flycatcher
Sulphur-bellied Flycatcher
Tropical Kingbird
Rose-throated Becard
Long-tailed Manakin
Mangrove Swallow
White-throated Magpie-Jay
Rufous & White Wren
Plain Wren
White-lored Gnatcatcher
Swainson's Thrush
Lesser Greenlet
Yellow Warbler
Gray-crowned Yellowthroat
Red-legged Honeycreeper
Scrub Euphonia
Summer Tanager
Grayish Saltator
Rose-breasted Grosbeak
Olive Sparrow
Yellow-faced Grassquit
Streak-backed Oriole

Collared Aracari
Hoffman's Woodpecker
Pale-billed Woodpecker
Streak-headed Woodcreeper
N. Beardless Tyrannulet
Greenish Elaenia
Yellow-olive Flycatcher
Bright-rumped Attila
Nutting's Flycatcher
Brown-crested Flycatcher
Boat-billed Flycatcher
Streaked Flycatcher
Piratic Flycatcher
Scissor-tailed Flycatcher
Masked Tityra
Gray-breasted Martin
Barn Swallow
Rufous-naped Wren
Banded Wren
House Wren
Clay-colored Thrush
Yellow-green Vireo
Tennessee Warbler
Northern Waterthrush
Rufous-capped Warbler
Thick-billed Euphonia
Blue-gray Tanager
Western Tanager
Buff-throated Saltator
Indigo Bunting
White-collared Seedeater
Northern Oriole

Barra Honda National Park

This park exists to control and protect some fine limestone caves but also has some interesting, if sparse, Tropical Dry Forest. You would probably need a guide to see the caves and will surely be approached by one. Howler monkeys are particularly easy to see here.

Access is via the Tempisque ferry and the highway to Nicoya with a well-signed road leading off to the right about 6 km west of the ferry. There are signs at the intersections. A small stream crosses the road near the park so you would probably need 4WD during the rainy season.

There is a small tourist project with a restaurant, camping, and some cabinas. The price to sleep indoors is 1000 Colones per person. This operation is struggling and may not be operating when you arrive, but it is right at the park entrance.

Ask at the park entrance for permission to enter early as the only trails go right by the building. Birding is good along any of the trails and the relatively sparse vegetation makes species like Thicket Tinamou, Lesser Ground Cuckoo, and Long-tailed Manakin easier to observe than elsewhere.

Birds of Barra Honda National Park

Thicket Tinamou
Gray Hawk
Plain Chachalaca
White-fronted Parrot
Lesser Ground-Cuckoo
Pacific Screech-Owl
Lesser Nighthawk
Steely-vented Hummingbird
Cinnamon Hummingbird
Black-headed Trogon
Turquoise-browed Motmot
Roadside Hawk
Broad-winged Hawk
Orange-fronted Parakeet
Inca Dove
Mangrove Cuckoo
Pauraque
Fork-tailed Emerald
Ruby-throated Hummingbird
Elegant Trogon
Blue-crowned Motmot
Hoffman's Woodpecker

Pale-billed Woodpecker
Streaked Flycatcher
Brown-crested Flycatcher
Long-tailed Manakin
Banded Wren
Yellow-throated Vireo
Lesser Greenlet
Rufous-capped Warbler
Yellow-olive Flycatcher
Nutting's Flycatcher
Great Crested Flycatcher
Rufous-naped Wren
White-lored Gnatcatcher
Yellow-green Vireo
Tennessee Warbler
Olive Sparrow

Beaches

It is possible to bird Guanacaste from one of the beach resorts that are springing up on the outer coast of the Nicoya peninsula. Habitat around the towns is not as good as in the national parks but the common species can be seen.

The best site with much infrastructure is probably Tamarindo, which in addition to dry forest and scrub has an estuary with mangroves. You can rent a boat in town to visit the mangroves, though most of the Pacific coast mangrove specialties don't range this far north. The estuary also has a few shorebirds.

Other areas that have at least some habitat and have a decent range of accommodation include Playa Hermosa and Playas del Coco near Liberia, and the Nosara/Samara area further south.

The
Mountains

The Mountains

The volcanic ranges that form the spine of Costa Rica are its most striking geographical feature and the source of most of its biological diversity. Many of the best sites are within easy reach of San José so it is possible to visit several without changing hotels.

A number of good areas are not covered here due to access problems. If you don't mind bad roads, Rincón de la Vieja National Park, on the volcano of the same name above Liberia, is well worth visiting. The area around Volcán Arenal is popular with tourists wanting to see the active volcano, but there is not too much habitat. Finally, a vast area of the Cordillera de Talamanca is protected by Chirripó and La Amistad National Parks, but the habitat types here are much more easily visited at Cerro de la Muerte.

The locations below are biased towards the Caribbean slope, in part because that's where the parks are but also because the middle-elevation Caribbean slope has a very distinctive avifauna with a substantial number of difficult-to-find species. It is well worth extra time. Also, much of the Pacific slope near the Valle Central has been extensively deforested.

Braulio Carrillo National Park

Long popular with birders for its good habitat within easy reach of San José, this park has suffered in recent years from a spate of car break-ins and armed robbery. Tourists with expensive cameras and binoculars are apparently the main target. For this reason the well-known Botella (Botarrama) trail is essentially off limits, though a newer trail by the lower park station partly replaces it for birding purposes. See the May 1994 issue of *Winging It* for what could happen if you believe the tourist brochures that say how nice Costa Ricans and don't heed this warning.

It is also possible to visit another corner of the park, above the town of Sacramento de Heredia. This requires a 4 km uphill hike along an undrivable road to get to the park boundary, then another few kilometers through good forest to a lake near the Volcán Barva. This would be an all-day outing.

Braulio Carrillo provides scenery unsurpassed in Costa Rica and a good transect of Caribbean slope forest. The main access is along the Guápiles highway, which starts out as Calle 3 northbound in San José. The first park station is about half an hour from the city, the second about 15 minutes further. Due to problems mentioned above, the only access is two trails where you can leave your car at the park stations. These spots are also readily reached by public transport, the best choice being the hourly Guápiles bus.

The first trail starts about 50 meters back towards San José and across the road from the first park station, just before the Zurquí tunnel. It is good for high-elevation species though you don't ever really escape traffic noise. The forest here is a bit scrubby but supports a good variety of birds.

At the other station by the Río Quebrada Gonzales, a loop trail goes into good foothill forest with a mix of middle- and low-elevation species. The station is not really obvious from the highway, so watch for the bridge. Local species like Yellow-eared Toucanet, Lattice-tailed Trogon, Purplish-backed Quail-Dove, and Ashy-throated Bush-Tanager can be found here.

Birds of Braulio Carrillo National Park

Great Tinamou
Highland Tinamou
White Hawk
Black-chested Hawk
Black Hawk-Eagle
Crested Guan
Black Guan
Rufous-fronted Wood-Quail
Black-breasted Wood-Quail
Sunbittern
Band-tailed Pigeon
Ruddy Pigeon
Short-billed Pigeon
Gray-chested Dove
Purplish-backed Quail-Dove
Buff-fronted Quail-Dove
Ruddy Quail-Dove
Chiriquí Quail-Dove

Crimson-fronted Parakeet
Brown-hooded Parrot
Vermiculated Screech-Owl
Andean Pygmy-Owl
Chestnut-collared Swift
Vaux's Swift
Green-fronted Lancebill
Long-tailed Hermit
Violet Sabrewing
Brown Violetear
Black-crested Coquette
Crowned Woodnymph
Rufous-tailed Hummingbird
White-bellied Mountain-gem
Green-crowned Brilliant
Scintillant Hummingbird
Slaty-tailed Trogon
Collared Trogon
Violaceous Trogon
Rufous Motmot
Prong-billed Barbet
Collared Aracari
Rufous-winged Woodpecker
Plain-brown Woodcreeper
Wedge-billed Woodcreeper
Black-banded Woodcreeper
Spotted Woodcreeper
Spot-crowned Woodcreeper
Red-faced Spinetail
Spotted Barbtail
Lineated Foliage-gleaner
Buff-fronted Foliage-gleaner
Streak-breasted Treehunter

Barred Parakeet
White-crowned Parrot
Spectacled Owl
White-collared Swift
Black Swift
Gray-rumped Swift
Green Hermit
White-tipped Sicklebill
Green Violetear
Violet-headed Hummingbird
Green Thorntail
Blue-throated Goldentail
Snowcap
Purple-throated Mountain-gem
Purple-crowned Fairy
Resplendent Quetzal
Lattice-tailed Trogon
Black-throated Trogon
Broad-billed Motmot
Red-headed Barbet
Emerald Toucanet
Yellow-eared Toucanet
Smoky-brown Woodpecker
Olivaceous Woodcreeper
Barred Woodcreeper
Black-striped Woodcreeper
Streak-headed Woodcreeper
Brown-billed Scythebill
Ruddy Treerunner
Striped Foliage-gleaner
Spectacled Foliage-gleaner
Buff-throated Foliage-gleaner
Plain Xenops

Gray-throated Leaftosser
Tawny-throated Leaftosser
Scaly-throated Leaftosser
Russet Antshrike
Slaty Antshrike
Plain Antvireo
Streak-crowned Antvireo
Checker-throated Antwren
Slaty Antwren
Dot-winged Antwren
Rufous-rumped Antwren
Chestnut-backed Antbird
Dull-mantled Antbird
Immaculate Antbird
Bicolored Antbird
Spotted Antbird
Black-headed Antthrush
Rufous-breasted Antthrush
Silvery-fronted Tapaculo
Red-capped Manakin
White-crowned Manakin
White-ruffed Manakin
Rufous Mourner
Rufous Piha
Cinnamon Becard
Barred Becard
White-winged Becard
Black & White Becard
Bare-necked Umbrellabird
Sharpbill
Golden-bellied Flycatcher
Dusky-capped Flycatcher
Dark Pewee
Yellowish Flycatcher
Tufted Flycatcher
Yellow-olive Flycatcher
Yellow-margined Flycatcher
Eye-ringed Flatbill
Northern Bentbill
Zeledon's Tyrannulet
Slaty-capped Flycatcher
Olive-striped Flycatcher
Ochre-bellied Flycatcher
Azure-hooded Jay
Stripe-breasted Wren
Bay Wren
White-breasted Wood-Wren
Gray-breasted Wood-Wren
Northern Nightingale-Wren
Song Wren
Pale-vented Thrush
Mountain Thrush
Black-faced Solitaire
Wood Thrush
Swainson's Thrush
Slaty-backed Nightingale-Thrush
Black-headed Nightingale-Thrush
Ruddy-capped Nightingale-Thrush
Tropical Gnatcatcher
Long-billed Gnatwren
Tawny-faced Gnatwren
Green Shrike-Vireo
Brown-capped Vireo
Lesser Greenlet
Bananaquit
Tropical Parula

Golden-crowned Warbler
Buff-rumped Warbler
Blue Dacnis
Emerald Tanager
Speckled Tanager
Rufous-winged Tanager
Golden-browed Chlorophonia
Tawny-capped Euphonia
Olive Tanager
White-shouldered Tanager
Scarlet-rumped Tanager
Sooty-capped Bush-Tanager
Black & Yellow Tanager
Sooty-faced Finch
Orange-billed Sparrow
Three-striped Warbler
Green Honeycreeper
Scarlet-thighed Dacnis
Silver-throated Tanager
Bay-headed Tanager
Spangle-cheeked Tanager
Blue-hooded Euphonia
Blue & Gold Tanager
Tawny-crested Tanager
Dusky-faced Tanager
Common Bush-Tanager
Ashy-throated Bush-Tanager
Rose-breasted Grosbeak
Chestnut-capped Brush-Finch

Tapantí National Park

This park preserves a watershed with superb Caribbean foothill forest. Access is easy with a car, very difficult by public transport. Park personnel are familiar with birders, so just drive by the station if you arrive before 8 and pay on the way out.

To arrive from San José, pass through Cartago to the town of Paraíso. The highway forces you into the center of town, where you make a right on Calle 2 towards the town of Orosí. Continue on the paved road through Orosí to an obvious electrical substation where the road goes straight and turns to broken asphalt, potholes, and mud if it has rained. It should nonetheless be passible with an ordinary car at any time. After about 7 km, there is a river crossing with good birding early in the morning. After a couple more km the park station is the first building on the right. From San José to the park is about a 1 1/2 hour drive. (Note: as of 1994 there were several culverts washed out on the

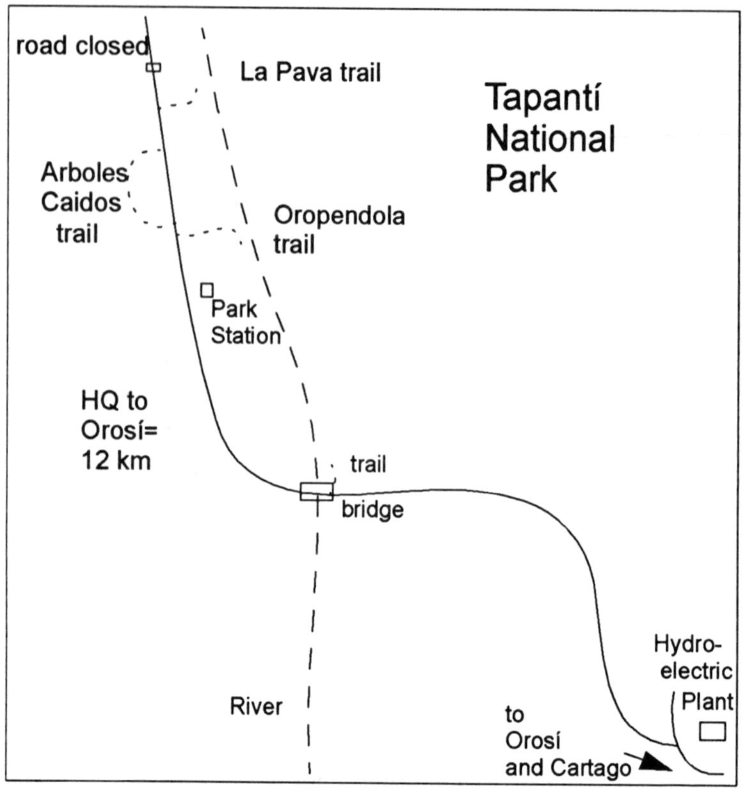

far side of Orosí, necessitating a small detour. It will probably be a dog's lifetime before this is fixed, so you may have to ask directions.)

The best birding is along a rather good gravel road that eventually leads to a hydroelectric plant on the mountain. The road is closed to vehicle traffic after about 5 km but you can and should walk it further. The several trails are good but less important. There is some general use and the road has been discovered by mountain bicyclists, but during the week you should have the place more or less to yourself.

Tapantí is readily reached as a day trip from San José but there are also a number of modest cabins in the Orosí valley. Right by the entrance is the Kiri Lodge with cabins for $15 for one person and $25 for two. There is a restaurant on the premises as well. Call 573-3040 for reservations (Spanish).

Birds of Tapantí

Black Guan
Band-tailed Pigeon
Brown-hooded Parrot
Vaux's Swift
Green-crowned Brilliant
Black-bellied Hummingbird
Purple-throated Mountain-gem
Collared Trogon
Red-headed Barbet
Red-faced Spinetail
Streaked Xenops
Slaty Antwren
Olive-striped Flycatcher
Tufted Flycatcher
Golden-bellied Flycatcher
Gray-breasted Wood-Wren
Black-faced Solitaire
N. Am. Dipper
Rufous-browed Peppershrike
Golden-winged Warbler
Black-throated Green Warbler
Black & White Warbler
Wilson's Warbler
Collared Whitestart
Three-striped Warbler
Silver-throated Tanager
Golden-hooded Tanager
Rufous-winged Tanager
Black-chested Hawk
Ruddy Pigeon
White-crowned Parrot
Green Hermit
Green-fronted Lancebill
White-bellied Mountain-gem
Green Thorntail
Emerald Toucanet
Prong-billed Barbet
Spotted Barbtail
Buffy Tuftedcheek
Paltry Tyrannulet
Dark Pewee
Black Phoebe
Bright-rumped Attila
Ochraceous Wren
Orange-billed Nightingale-Thrush
Brown-capped Vireo
Tennessee Warbler
Blackburnian Warbler
Chestnut-sided Warbler
Mourning Warbler
Slate-throated Whitestart
Tropical Parula
Scarlet-thighed Dacnis
Spangle-cheeked Tanager
Bay-headed Tanager
White-winged Tanager

Common Bush-Tanager	Golden-browed Chlorophonia
Tawny-capped Euphonia	Blue-hooded Euphonia
Scarlet-rumped Tanager	Crimson-collared Tanager
Sooty-faced Finch	Yellow-throated Brush-Finch
Yellow-faced Grassquit	Variable Seedeater
Rufous-collared Sparrow	Lesser Goldfinch

Volcán Irazú National Park

The primary attraction here is a barren volcanic crater at the top of a rather large mountain, with views to both coasts on a clear day. It is easily reached from San José via Cartago.

To reach the park from San José, take the freeway to Cartago. Ignore the set of signs saying "Volcan Irazu" and continue to the main entrance to Cartago, where two lanes of the road curve left and one continues straight towards Cerro de la Muerte and San Isidro. You will shortly find yourself on Avenida 2, follow it a few blocks, and turn left just after a large church following signs for the Volcan. It is a long climb up through the towns of Cot, Llano Grande, and Tierra Blanca, set amidst the main vegetable-growing area of the country.

For slightly lower elevation birding, turn left at a paved road with signs for Prussia, and bird the roadside for a few km until it dead-ends at a park. The forest at the far end of the road is mostly exotic and doesn't support many birds but along the road are many Green Violetears etc. This can be good on a cold day as you wait for things to warm up a bit at the summit.

The vegetation at the top has not had much time to grow back from the most recent eruption (1963) but supports lots of Volcano Hummingbirds and other species. The parking lot usually has Volcano Junco.

Just below the park gate a road goes off to the right and down the north side of the mountain into additional interesting habitat. The road is steep in places but should be passible with an ordinary car.

Birds of Irazú National Park & vicinity

Buffy-crowned Wood-Partridge
Band-tailed Pigeon
White-collared Swift
Fiery-throated Hummingbird
Volcano Hummingbird
Mountain Elaenia
Blue & White Swallow
Sooty Thrush
Flame-throated Warbler
Slate-throated Whitestart
Sooty-capped Bush-Tanager
Yellow-thighed Finch
Volcano Junco
Red-billed Pigeon
Mourning Dove
Green Violetear
Scintillant Hummingbird
Acorn Woodpecker
Black-capped Flycatcher
Black-billed Nightingale-Thrush
Long-tailed Silky-Flycatcher
Wilson's Warbler
Flame-colored Tanager
Large-footed Finch
Rufous-collared Sparrow

Guayabo National Monument

This park preserves the most significant pre-Colombian archeological site in Costa Rica. Though not up to the standards of Mesoamerican civilizations further north, it is worth a visit. Most of the forest is not more than 30 years old but the road and campground always seem to have an impressive variety of wintering birds.

To reach the monument, proceed to the town of Turrialba. A couple of blocks after entering the town, a sign directs you to turn left for Santa Rosa and Guayabo. The bridge you want is actually a block or so back to the left from the street you are on, so take the last possibility (all one way) and cross the one-lane bridge that looks like a railroad bridge. Don't go towards Santa Rosa after the initial turn. Across the bridge, continue on the paved road until a sign directs you up a gravel road to the monument.

There is camping at the monument but it often rains. Nearby on the entrance road, there is a small hotel with a restaurant. There is also a soda within walking distance of the reserve.

The trails through the second-growth around the archeological area are heavily supervised, as they don't want visitors doing impromptu excavations for that overlooked piece of gold. The best birding is usually along the road anyway. There are also some very steep trails down to the river through primary forest but they are not being maintained. About a kilometer upstream is a very nice waterfall with nesting Dippers; get directions locally, as this requires a long cross-country hike.

The grounds of CATIE, an agricultural experimental station east of Turrialba on the road to Síquirres, can be good. There is a pond where one can easily see Jacanas, etc. Ask permission at the gate.

Birds of Guayabo National Monument

Little Tinamou
Cattle Egret
Turkey Vulture
Black Vulture
Double-toothed Kite
Black Hawk-Eagle
Gray-headed Chachalaca
Red-billed Pigeon
Short-billed Pigeon
Ruddy Ground-Dove
White-tipped Dove
Crimson-fronted Parakeet
White-crowned Parrot
Squirrel Cuckoo
Groove-billed Ani
Pauraque
White-collared Swift
Vaux's Swift
Green Hermit
Violet Sabrewing
Green-crowned Brilliant
Green Violetear
Rufous-tailed Hummingbird
Crowned Woodnymph
Purple-crowned Fairy
Violaceous Trogon
Broad-billed Motmot
Rufous Motmot
Blue-crowned Motmot
Red-headed Barbet
Keel-billed Toucan
Collared Aracari

Emerald Toucanet
Golden-olive Woodpecker
Pale-billed Woodpecker
Olivaceous Woodcreeper
Buff-throated Woodcreeper
Plain Xenops
White-fringed Antwren
White-ruffed Manakin
Rufous Mourner
Black-crowned Tityra
Great Kiskadee
Piratic Flycatcher
Tropical Pewee
Slaty-capped Flycatcher
Yellow-olive Flycatcher
Olive-striped Flycatcher
Blue & White Swallow
Band-backed Wren
Canebrake Wren
House Wren
Clay-colored Thrush
Yellow-throated Vireo
Brown-capped Vireo
Bananaquit
Green Honeycreeper
Golden-winged Warbler
Tropical Parula
Chestnut-sided Warbler
Mourning Warbler
Slate-throated Whitestart
Rufous-capped Warbler
Montezuma Oropendola
Tawny-capped Euphonia

Black-cheeked Woodpecker
Rufous-winged Woodpecker
Lineated Woodpecker
Streak-headed Woodcreeper
Spectacled Foliage-gleaner
Barred Antshrike
Black-faced Antthrush
Cinnamon Becard
Masked Tityra
Tropical Kingbird
Social Flycatcher
Dusky-capped Flycatcher
Yellowish Flycatcher
Eye-ringed Flatbill
Paltry Tyrannulet
Ochre-bellied Flycatcher
Brown Jay
Stripe-breasted Wren
Bay Wren
Gray-breasted Wood-Wren
Tropical Gnatcatcher
Yellow-green Vireo
Lesser Greenlet
Scarlet-thighed Dacnis
Black & White Warbler
Tennessee Warbler
Blackburnian Warbler
Kentucky Warbler
Wilson's Warbler
Golden-crowned Warbler
Buff-rumped Warbler
Giant Cowbird
Olive-backed Euphonia

Silver-throated Tanager
Bay-headed Tanager
Palm Tanager
Crimson-collared Tanager
Flame-colored Tanager
Black-headed Saltator
Rose-breasted Grosbeak
Yellow-throated Brush-Finch
Rufous-collared Sparrow
Golden-masked Tanager
Blue-gray Tanager
Scarlet-rumped Tanager
Summer Tanager
White-shouldered Tanager
Buff-throated Saltator
Yellow-faced Grassquit
Orange-billed Sparrow

Volcán Poás National Park

This popular national park offers an active volcano and some good high-elevation habitat. It is well-visited by both Ticos and foreign tourists so arrive early and avoid weekends.

The park is readily reached via Alajuela or Heredia. These towns have a confusing array of one-way streets that you will have to find your way through. Generally you want to exit the opposite corner of town. Get a map first.

If you arrive before the gate opens in the morning, there is plenty of habitat along the main road and a dirt road that goes off to the left (just below the gate) towards a small tourist development. As with Volcán Irazú, there are relatively few species here but they tend to be high-mountain specialties.

Birds of Volcán Poás National Park

Swallow-tailed Kite
Barred Hawk
Spotted Wood-Quail
Barred Parakeet
Red-tailed Hawk
Black Guan
Band-tailed Pigeon
Bare-shanked Screech-Owl

Dusky Nightjar
White-collared Swift
Vaux's Swift
Green Violetear
Fiery-throated Hummingbird
Magnificent Hummingbird
Volcano Hummingbird
Scintillant Hummingbird
Resplendent Quetzal
Collared Trogon
Emerald Toucanet
Acorn Woodpecker
Hairy Woodpecker
Spot-crowned Woodcreeper
Ruddy Treerunner
Buffy Tuftedcheek
Silvery-fronted Tapaculo
Black-capped Flycatcher
Mountain Elaenia
Blue & White Swallow
Ochraceous Wren
Gray-breasted Wood-Wren
Sooty Thrush
Mountain Thrush
Ruddy-capped Nightingale-Thrush
Black-billed Nightingale-Thrush
Long-tailed Silky-Flycatcher
Black & Yellow Silky-Flycatcher
Yellow-winged Vireo
Brown-capped Vireo
Slaty Flower-piercer
Flame-throated Warbler
Black-throated Green Warbler
Wilson's Warbler
Collared Whitestart
Black-cheeked Warbler
Wrenthrush
Sooty-capped Bush-Tanager
Large-footed Finch
Sooty-faced Finch
Yellow-thighed Finch
Rufous-collared Sparrow

Virgen del Socorro

Good lower foothill forest can be accessed from the Sarapiquí highway at the Virgen del Socorro forest reserve. Birding is from a rough dirt road that crosses the Sarapiquí river and doubles back up the other side of the canyon to some farms on the opposite ridge.

The entrance to the forest reserve is about 4 km below the El Angel marmalade factory below Varablanca, about one long hour from San José via Heredia. The road is the first turn on the right after the factory, and requires a sharp right turn. If driving a 4WD vehicle, be careful not to heat up your brakes on the long curving decent from the pass.

Birding is good along the road in both directions from the bridge. A good trail with some additional species goes upstream along the river about 50 feet from the bridge on the highway side. Conditions are more difficult along the trail due to the closed canopy and water noise.

Birds of Virgen del Socorro

Swallow-tailed Kite	Black-chested Hawk
Broad-winged Hawk	Bat Falcon
Crimson-fronted Parakeet	White-crowned Parrot
Squirrel Cuckoo	White-collared Swift
Vaux's Swift	Green Hermit
Little Hermit	Brown Violetear
Violet-headed Hummingbird	Crowned Woodnymph
Coppery-headed Emerald	Green Thorntail
Green-crowned Brilliant	Purple-crowned Fairy
Collared Trogon	Collared Aracari
Red-headed Barbet	Prong-billed Barbet
Smoky-brown Woodpecker	Rufous-winged Woodpecker
Spotted Woodcreeper	Streak-headed Woodcreeper
Red-faced Spinetail	Spotted Barbtail
Immaculate Antbird	Slaty Antwren
Paltry Tyrannulet	Torrent Tyrannulet
Rufous-browed Tyrannulet	Slaty-capped Flycatcher
Scale-crested Pygmy-Tyrant	Yellow-margined Flycatcher
Tufted Flycatcher	Yellow-bellied Flycatcher
Golden-bellied Flycatcher	White-ruffed Manakin
Azure-hooded Jay	Bay Wren
Northern Nightingale Wren	N. Am. Dipper
Tawny-faced Gnatwren	Slaty-backed Nightingale-Thrush

Wood Thrush	Pale-vented Thrush
Yellow-throated Vireo	Lesser Greenlet
Tropical Parula	Golden-winged Warbler
Black-throated Green Warbler	Black & White Warbler
Chestnut-sided Warbler	Blackburnian Warbler
Kentucky Warbler	Mourning Warbler
Wilson's Warbler	Slate-throated Whitestart
Three-striped Warbler	Golden-crowned Warbler
Bananaquit	Emerald Tanager
Silver-throated Tanager	Bay-headed Tanager
Speckled Tanager	Scarlet-thighed Dacnis
Tawny-capped Euphonia	Crimson-collared Tanager
Scarlet-rumped Tanager	Common Bush-Tanager
Black & Yellow Tanager	Slate-colored Grosbeak
Rose-breasted Grosbeak	Sooty-faced Finch

Cerro de la Muerte

Crossing the Cerro de la Muerte, the Pan-American Highway reaches its highest point. The highway provides easy access to a range of habitats, including high-elevation oak forest and a type of shrubby brushlands similar to the Andean páramo. Weather is often a problem here even in the dry season. Birding can still be good in a light rain or fog, but much wind can ruin your day.

Access is easy from San José, as all sites are near the highway and the far end can be reached in 100 minutes of cautious driving. Slides and sunken grades reduce the highway to one lane in a number of places. The highway is marked with concrete kilometer posts painted yellow; enough of them are still in view to provide a ready reference to your position. These will be referred to regularly in the following account.

The first point of reference is the Abastador La Trinidad at Km 63,

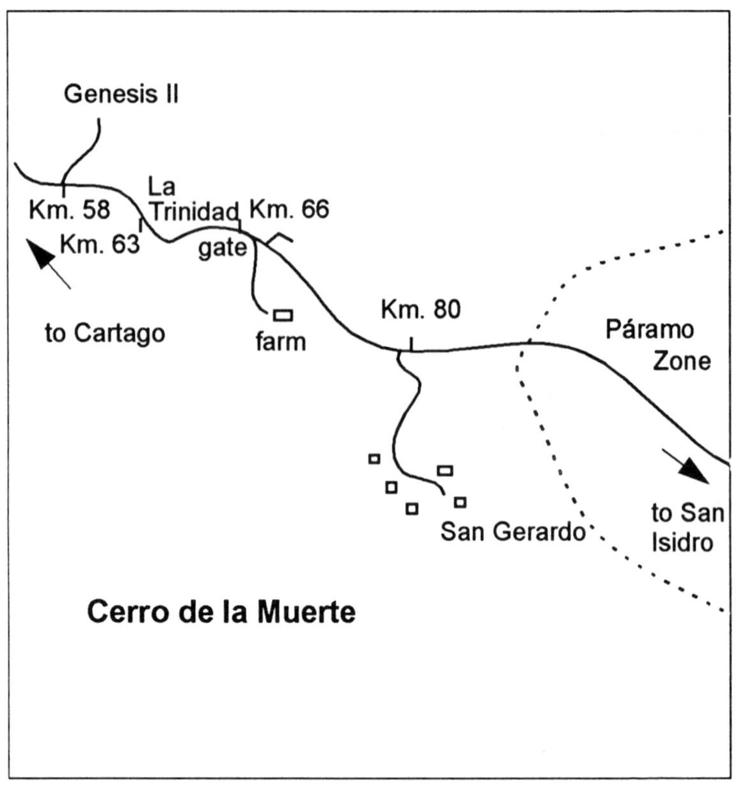

where the key to the gate allowing you access to the nice oak forest at Km 66 is kept. Entrance costs 600 Colones per person but is worth it for the Resplendent Quetzal and other species present. The road itself is on the right and has a black gate with a small green plaque telling you to go to the pulpería if you want the key. Just up the highway on the other side a dirt road goes off to some electric towers through some smaller forest, with good patches of brush and bamboo for Silvery-fronted Tapaculo, Black-billed Nightingale-Thrush and other high-elevation specialties. With considerable luck, Silvery-throated Jay might be found in this area.

At Km 80 a gravel road goes down to the right 8 km to San Gerardo. There are several hotels at the end of the road; the most expensive has trails into good Quetzal habitat. Otherwise there is some good birding along the road.

Around Km 88 the páramo zone is reached and the pass is shortly thereafter. Here, if conditions are good, you might find Timberline Wren, Wrenthrush, Volcano Hummingbird, and Volcano Junco.

Around Villa Mills at about Km 95 the road has started back down towards the Valle de General and the forest gets taller where it hasn't been converted into pasture. Anywhere you can find habitat is worth birding.

At Km 58 is the entrance to Genesis II, a private forest reserve. The house is about 4 km from the highway with every intersection well-marked. Admission to similar habitat as at Km 66 is $7.50. Accommodations are available as well.

Birds of Cerro de la Muerte

Highland Tinamou
Swallow-tailed Kite
Red-tailed Hawk
Band-tailed Pigeon
Buff-fronted Quail-Dove
Sulphur-winged Parakeet
Barred Parakeet
White-crowned Parrot
Andean Pygmy-Owl
Bare-shanked Screech-Owl
Dusky Nightjar
Green Violetear
Fiery-throated Hummingbird
White-throated Mountain-gem
Magnificent Hummingbird
Volcano Hummingbird
Collared Trogon
Resplendent Quetzal
Prong-billed Barbet
Emerald Toucanet
Acorn Woodpecker
Hairy Woodpecker
Ruddy Treerunner
Streak-breasted Treehunter
Spot-crowned Woodcreeper
Silvery-fronted Tapaculo
Golden-bellied Flycatcher
Zeledon's Tyrannulet
Mountain Elaenia
Yellowish Flycatcher
Black-capped Flycatcher
Tufted Flycatcher

Dark Pewee
Ochraceous Pewee
Blue & White Swallow
Silvery-throated Jay
Ochraceous Wren
House Wren
Timberline Wren
Gray-breasted Wood-Wren
Black-billed Nightingale-Thrush
Ruddy-capped Nightingale-Thrush
Mountain Thrush
Sooty Thrush
Black & Yellow Silky-Flycatcher
Long-tailed Silky-Flycatcher
Yellow-winged Vireo
Brown-capped Vireo
Rufous-browed Peppershrike
Flame-throated Warbler
Black-throated Green Warbler
Wilson's Warbler
Slate-throated Whitestart
Collared Whitestart
Black-cheeked Warbler
Wrenthrush
Common Bush-Tanager
Sooty-capped Bush-Tanager
Yellow-thighed Finch
Large-footed Finch
Peg-billed Finch
Slaty Flower-piercer
Rufous-collared Sparrow
Eastern Meadowlark

San Vito area

Situated near the Panama border, San Vito has a number of species more typical of the Zona Sur as well as good mid-elevation birding. Most of the area is cut-over but birding is good in second-growth and at the Las Cruces Botanical Gardens.

San Vito is about 300 km from San José, or about five to six hours driving time over the Cerro de la Muerte, through San Isidro, and across the bridge at Paso Real to town. Driving time depends on conditions on the Cerro.

There are a variety of hotels in San Vito or you can stay at the OTS research facility at Las Cruces. High season rates with meals are $79 per person in the cabins or $58 in the bunkrooms. A day visit to the gardens

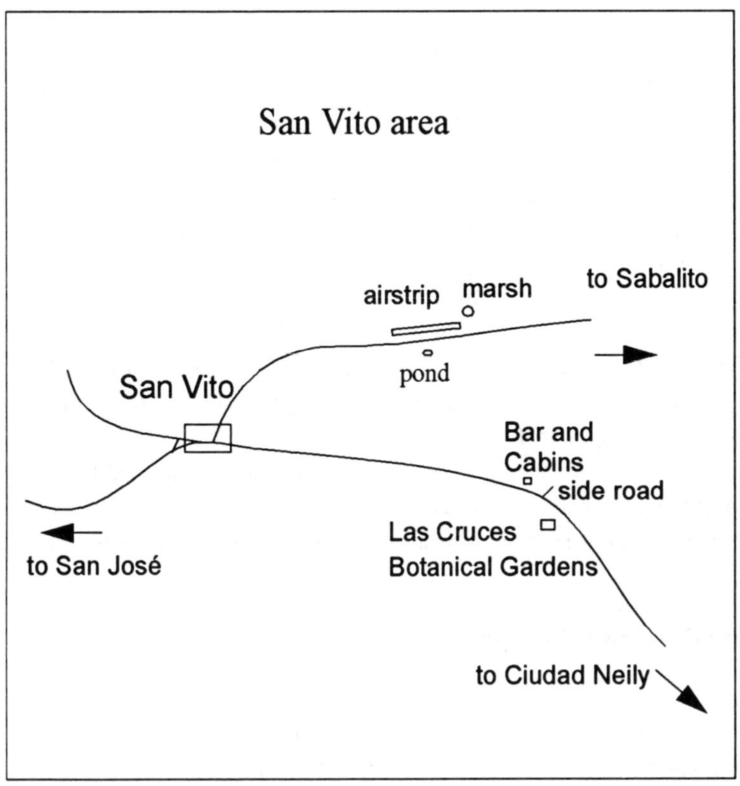

and adjacent forest reserve is $6. Don't book the day trip with OTS in San José as they will charge much more. For reservations:

WBG, Apt. 73
San Vito de Java
Coto Brus
Costa Rica
Tel. & fax: 773-3278

There is also a small bar and restaurant about a kilometer back towards San Vito. They have some rather basic cabinas for about $15 per person.

Of considerable interest are some ponds near the San Vito airport on the road to Sabalito. Arriving from Paso Real at the five-way intersection in San Vito, take the road straight across the intersection to the right of the La Ceiba hotel. After a few kilometers the unused airstrip will appear on the left. There is one pond about halfway down it, then a small wetlands reserve off the far end. Walk along the path between two houses to get to the park and observation tower. Specialties here include Masked Duck, Pale-breasted Spinetail, and Masked (Chiriquí) Yellowthroat.

Birding is also excellent around the Las Cruces gardens, though you don't actually have to go in to see good birds. From the five-way intersection in San Vito, take the right fork about 5 km to the gardens. The well-tended gardens and the trails through the OTS reserve are well worth working, but if you don't want to pay the six bucks, a dirt road about 400 meters back towards San Vito and across the road has been very productive in the past. This road leads about 300 meters to a small *campesino* house whose occupants are unconcerned about birdwatchers.

Birds of San Vito area

Green Heron
Blue-winged Teal
Masked Duck
Swallow-tailed Kite
White-throated Crake
Common Moorhen
Purple Gallinule
Scaled Pigeon
Crimson-fronted Parakeet
Orange-chinned Parakeet
White-crowned Parrot
Striped Cuckoo
Vaux's Swift
Little Hermit
Rufous-tailed Hummingbird
Long-billed Starthroat
Blue-crowned Motmot
Violaceous Trogon
Red-crowned Woodpecker
Pale-breasted Spinetail
Buff-throated Foliage-gleaner
Ruddy Foliage-gleaner
Buff-throated Woodcreeper
Streak-headed Woodcreeper
Russet Antshrike
Plain Antvireo

Slaty Antwren
Lesser Elaenia
Ochre-bellied Flycatcher
Common Tody-Flycatcher
Golden-crowned Spadebill
Dusky-capped Flycatcher
White-ruffed Manakin
Plain Wren
Slaty-backed Nightingale-Thrush
White-throated Thrush
Tropical Parula
Kentucky Warbler
Wilson's Warbler
Bananaquit
Speckled Tanager
Golden-hooded Tanager
Blue Dacnis
Thick-billed Euphonia
Red-crowned Ant-Tanager
Common Bush-Tanager
Buff-throated Saltator
Orange-billed Sparrow
Blue-black Grassquit
Yellow-faced Grassquit
Paltry Tyrannulet
Yellow-bellied Elaenia
Scale-crested Pygmy-Tyrant
Yellow-olive Flycatcher
Bright-rumped Attila
Piratic Flycatcher
Rufous-breasted Wren
Southern Nightingale-Wren
Clay-colored Thrush
Golden-winged Warbler
American Redstart
Masked Yellowthroat
Rufous-capped Warbler
Silver-throated Tanager
Bay-headed Tanager
Scarlet-thighed Dacnis
Green Honeycreeper
Blue-gray Tanager
Summer Tanager
Streaked Saltator
Black-headed Brush-Finch
Black-striped Sparrow
Variable Seedeater

Monteverde Biological Reserve

Monteverde has established itself as one of the premier natural history destinations in Costa Rica, and for that reason you may want to skip it. Overconstruction of hotels, restaurants, and gift shops, high prices, a bad road, and often-inclement weather make it hard to recommend.

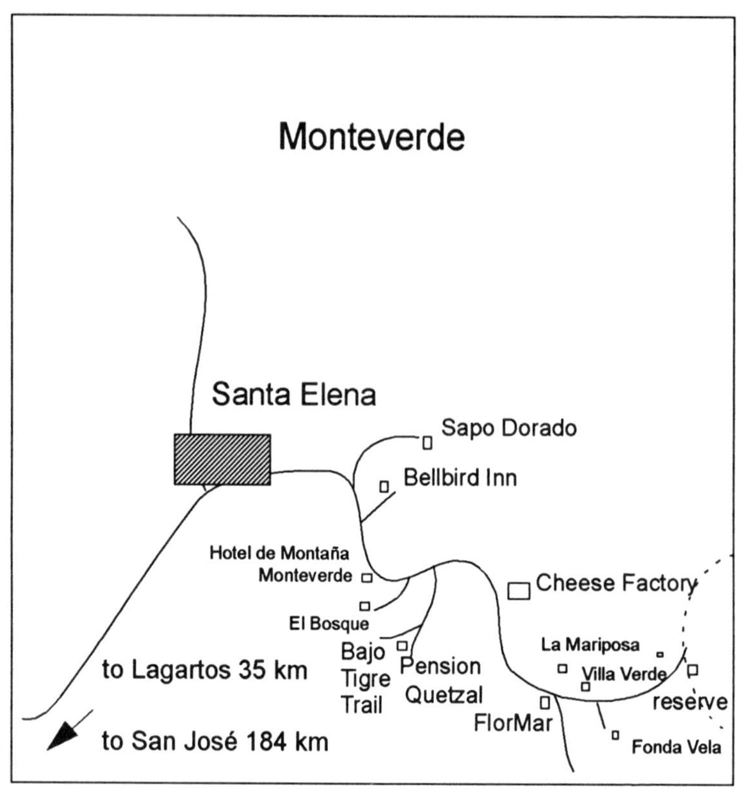

Santa Elena and the town of Monteverde are about 180 km from San José, or about 3 hours. The last 35 km is over a very rough road, allegedly kept that way by local interests to discourage day-tripping from San José or the beaches. Keep an eye on your tires, and if you get a flat you can get it fixed in Santa Elena. Just before Santa Elena there is a voluntary toll booth where you can give them 100 Colones for the maintenance of the road if you feel like it. There is also a useful map where the road to Monteverde takes off.

There is now quite a variety of hotels between Santa Elena and the reserve, ranging in price from about $7 to $70. Be aware that the cheapest places are mostly in Santa Elena, about 7 km from the reserve entrance. Construction has apparently outstripped demand so you shouldn't have a problem without reservations even in the high season.

The reserve itself, run by the Tropical Science Center, was one of the original non-governmental attempts at conservation in the country. It is a magnificent piece of cloud forest with several discernible habitats. It also costs $8 to get in. No more than 125 people are permitted in the reserve at any one time, so there is a remote possibility you might have to wait by the hummingbird feeders for a while. There are more hummingbird feeders by the gallery just down the road. Boot rental is also available, and the reserve runs refuges for hikers in the Peñas Blancas valley. They are 3 and 6 hours hiking time from the headquarters and cost $3.50 per person.

Birds of Monteverde

Black-chested Hawk	Swallow-tailed Kite
Barred Forest-Falcon	Black Guan
Black-breasted Wood-Quail	Band-tailed Pigeon
Ruddy Pigeon	Buff-fronted Quail-Dove
Chiriquí Quail-Dove	White-tipped Dove
Brown-hooded Parrot	Red-lored Parrot
Squirrel Cuckoo	Bare-shanked Screech-Owl
Mottled Owl	Chestnut-collared Swift
Vaux's Swift	White-collared Swift
Coppery-headed Emerald	Fiery-throated Hummingbird
Green-crowned Brilliant	Green Hermit
Green Violetear	Magenta-throated Woodstar
Magnificent Hummingbird	Purple-throated Mountain-gem
Scintillant Hummingbird	Stripe-tailed Hummingbird
Violet Sabrewing	Orange-bellied Trogon
Resplendent Quetzal	Prong-billed Barbet
Emerald Toucanet	Golden-olive Woodpecker

Hairy Woodpecker	Smoky-brown Woodpecker
Olivaceous Woodcreeper	Spotted Woodcreeper
Streak-headed Woodcreeper	Buffy Tuftedcheek
Lineated Foliage-gleaner	Red-faced Spinetail
Ruddy Treerunner	Spotted Barbtail
Streak-breasted Treehunter	Immaculate Antbird
Slaty Antwren	Silvery-fronted Tapaculo
Long-tailed Manakin	Bright-rumped Attila
Masked Tityra	Three-wattled Bellbird
Dark Pewee	Dusky-capped Flycatcher
Mountain Elaenia	Olive-striped Flycatcher
Paltry Tyrannulet	Sulphur-bellied Flycatcher
Tufted Flycatcher	Yellowish Flycatcher
White-throated Spadebill	Blue & White Swallow
N. Rough-winged Swallow	S. Rough-winged Swallow
Azure-hooded Jay	Brown Jay
Gray-breasted Wood-Wren	Ochraceous Wren
Rufous & White Wren	House Wren
Black-faced Solitaire	Black-headed Nightingale-Thrush
Orange-billed Nightingale-Thrush	Slaty-backed Nightingale-Thrush
Ruddy-capped Nightingale-Thrush	Swainson's Thrush
Clay-colored Thrush	Mountain Thrush
White-throated Thrush	Black & Yellow Silky-Flycatcher
Rufous-browed Peppershrike	Brown-capped Vireo
Yellow-green Vireo	Lesser Greenlet
Slaty Flower-piercer	Scarlet-thighed Dacnis
Black & White Warbler	Black-throated Green Warbler
Townsend's Warbler	Golden-winged Warbler
Blackburnian Warbler	Canada Warbler
Wilson's Warbler	Collared Whitestart
Slate-throated Whitestart	Golden-crowned Warbler
Three-striped Warbler	Wrenthrush
Eastern Meadowlark	Northern Oriole

Golden-browed Chlorophonia
Sooty-capped Bush-Tanager
Silver-throated Tanager
Yellow-throated Euphonia
Buff-throated Saltator
Yellow-throated Brush-Finch
Yellow-thighed Finch
Rufous-collared Sparrow

Common Bush-Tanager
Hepatic Tanager
Spangle-cheeked Tanager
Black-thighed Grosbeak
Chestnut-capped Brush-Finch
Sooty-faced Finch
White-eared Ground-Sparrow
Yellow-faced Grassquit

The Atlantic Lowlands

The Atlantic Lowlands

The Atlantic slope of Costa Rica, until recently mostly forest, is being converted to cattle pasture and banana plantations with alarming speed. Despite the amount of the country it represents, there are few good, easily-accessible birding spots. Some of the more-interesting species can also be seen at Caribbean foothill localities in the mountain section.

Most of the avifauna of the Caribbean lowlands is widespread, so if you have spent time in eastern Mexico or lowland South America this area might be low priority. It is essential for a big list though, and the beaches are very nice.

Finca La Selva

Owned by OTS, a consortium of universities dedicated to research on the workings of the tropical rain forest, La Selva offers much for the birder though it is not a tourist facility. Prices are high and access is limited but it's worth the trouble.

La Selva is near the town of Puerto Viejo de Sarapiquí in Heredia province. (Don't confuse this with Puerto Viejo on the coast.) Access is via the Braulio Carrillo highway and a paved road to Horquetas and Puerto Viejo. The nearby Selva Verde Lodge is a possible source of more-affordable accommodations but is not affiliated with the reserve and cannot guarantee access.

Accommodation at the research station is mostly in dormitory style rooms and meals are in the cafeteria. Prices for 1995 will be about $100 per night, with three meals included. A more economical solution if you have transport is to stay in Puerto Viejo and pay $21 per person for a day visit, lunch included. There are a variety of hotels in Puerto Viejo. The gate opens at 6 a.m. though there may not be anyone available to check you in until much later than that. In either case you must make advance reservations with the Organization for Tropical Studies, and space is limited. If you wish to stay at the station, be sure that your reservation is for dinner, breakfast, and lunch the next day to guarantee access to the forest in the morning; otherwise an arriving group might have priority over you. Schedule this visit first and design the rest of your trip around it.

Organization For Tropical Studies
(from outside Costa Rica)
Interlink 341
Box 025635
Miami, Fl, 33152
(506) 240-6696

The reserve has an excellent trail system and a huge birdlist. Upon check-in you will get a map showing trails and areas with active research projects to avoid. The area around the station itself is excellent in the early morning, but for variety it is essential to spend as much time as possible working the forest. Tape recorders will most likely be banned soon, and birding can be difficult. Persistence will pay off here.

Birds of La Selva

Great Tinamou
Little Tinamou
Slaty-breasted Tinamou
Broad-winged Hawk
Semiplumbeous Hawk
Black Hawk-Eagle
Crested Guan
White-throated Crake
Sungrebe
Short-billed Pigeon
Gray-chested Dove
Olive-backed Quail-Dove
Olive-throated Parakeet
Crimson-fronted Parakeet
White-crowned Parrot
Brown-hooded Parrot
Red-lored Parrot
Mealy Parrot
Squirrel Cuckoo
Vermiculated Screech-Owl
Spectacled Owl
Least Pygmy-Owl
Pauraque
White-collared Swift
Gray-rumped Swift
L. Swallow-tailed Swift

Bronzy Hermit
Little Hermit
Crowned Woodnymph
Snowcap
Slaty-tailed Trogon
Violaceous Trogon
Broad-billed Motmot
Rufous-tailed Jacamar
White-whiskered Puffbird
Collared Aracari
Chestnut-mandibled Toucan
Chestnut-colored Woodpecker
Black-cheeked Woodpecker
Plain-brown Woodcreeper
Barred Woodcreeper
Black-striped Woodcreeper
Slaty Spinetail
Great Antshrike
Streak-crowned Antvireo
Checker-throated Antwren
Chestnut-backed Antbird
Fulvous-bellied Antpitta
Snowy Cotinga
Rufous Piha
Cinnamon Becard
Masked Tityra
Red-capped Manakin
Long-tailed Tyrant
Tropical Pewee
Ruddy-tailed Flycatcher
Black-headed Tody-Flycatcher
Slate-headed Tody-Flycatcher
Northern Bentbill

Long-tailed Hermit
White-necked Jacobin
Blue-chested Hummingbird
Red-footed Plumeleteer
Black-throated Trogon
Green Kingfisher
Rufous Motmot
Pied Puffbird
White-fronted Nunbird
Keel-billed Toucan
Rufous-winged Woodpecker
Cinnamon Woodpecker
Pale-billed Woodpecker
Wedge-billed Woodcreeper
Buff-throated Woodcreeper
Streak-headed Woodcreeper
Buff-throated Foliage-Gleaner
Slaty Antshrike
White-flanked Antwren
Dusky Antbird
Black-faced Antthrush
Spectacled Antpitta
Bright-rumped Attila
Rufous Mourner
White winged Becard
Purple-throated Fruitcrow
White-collared Manakin
White-ringed Flycatcher
Yellow-bellied Flycatcher
Golden-crowned Spadebill
Common Tody-Flycatcher
Yellow-margined Flycatcher
Black-capped Pygmy-Tyrant

Paltry Tyrannulet
Ochre-bellied Flycatcher
Bay Wren
White-breasted Wood-Wren
Tropical Gnatcatcher
Tawny-faced Gnatwren
Lesser Greenlet
Shining Honeycreeper
Blackburnian Warbler
Northern Waterthrush
Kentucky Warbler
Gray-crowned Yellowthroat
Montezuma Oropendola
Yellow-billed Cacique
Olive-backed Euphonia
Golden-hooded Tanager
Summer Tanager
Tawny-crested Tanager
Dusky-faced Tanager
Buff-throated Saltator
Blue-black Grosbeak
Variable Seedeater
Black-striped Sparrow
Slate-colored Grosbeak
Brown-capped Tyrannulet
Band-backed Wren
Stripe-breasted Wren
Song Wren
Long-billed Gnatwren
Green Shrike-Vireo
Tawny-crowned Greenlet
Bananaquit
Chestnut-sided Warbler
Ovenbird
Olive-crowned Yellowthroat
Buff-rumped Warbler
Scarlet-rumped Cacique
Yellow-crowned Euphonia
Plain-colored Tanager
Crimson-collared Tanager
Olive Tanager
Red-throated Ant-Tanager
Black-headed Saltator
Black-faced Grosbeak
Yellow-faced Grassquit
Thick-billed Seed-Finch
Orange-billed Sparrow

Cahuita and Puerto Viejo

The Caribbean coast south of Limón provides an easily accessible introduction to the birds of the Atlantic slope without the expense or hassle of some of the other areas. The well-developed tourist areas of Cahuita and Puerto Viejo are the obvious centers for exploration.

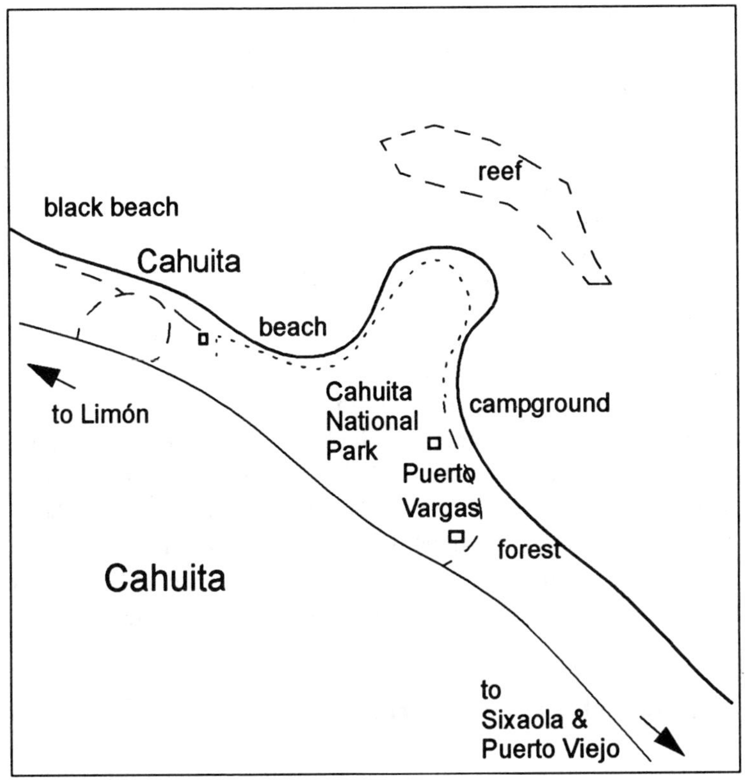

Though some distance apart, they will be combined here as their birdlife is similar.

Both areas are readily reached by the coastal strand highway that begins in Limón. It is the first main road, just before the docks as you enter town from San José. Maybe the sign there for Cahuita and the airport will be replaced someday. Via the Braulio Carrillo highway Limón is about a 2 1/2 hour drive from San José. Along the 43 km drive from Limón to Cahuita there are several river mouths that can have a few shorebirds, terns, etc. in season. The town itself is about a kilometer off the highway towards the ocean so watch for signs. There is a wide variety of accommodation available in Cahuita. Camping is available on the

Puerto Vargas side of the park but due to problems of theft and assault is not recommended unless you are on an extremely low budget.

Much of the best birding in the area is from the highway, with abundant open-country species and some local specialties like Nicaraguan Seed-Finch and Blue-headed Parrot. The Cahuita National Park is primarily a marine park, and doesn't have much in the way of trails except for one along the beach from Cahuita town to Puerto Vargas. There is one short trail inland starting just inside the park boundary on the Cahuita side. The road to Puerto Vargas and the campground goes through some nice forest.

Sixteen km further down the road is Puerto Viejo, popular with foreign tourists and surfers. Hotels of all shapes are springing up everywhere in town and along the road to Manzanillo. Prices are mostly modest. Birding here in generally similar to Cahuita, especially along the road to Manzanillo or Punta Mona. Of interest here are the abandoned cacao plantations in the hills above town, most of which are being filled with houses as the growth of tourism brings in more people. A good trail leaves from the southwest corner of the soccer field on the back side of town. Other trails might be located with local inquiry.

Birds of Cahuita and Puerto Viejo

Little Tinamou
Common Black-Hawk
Broad-winged Hawk
Gray-headed Chachalaca
White-throated Crake
Gray-necked Wood-Rail
Northern Jacana
Royal Tern
Pale-vented Pigeon
Short-billed Pigeon
Blue Ground-Dove
White-tipped Dove
Gray-chested Dove
Olive-backed Quail-Dove
Crimson-fronted Parakeet
Blue-headed Parrot
Mealy Parrot
Squirrel Cuckoo
Gray-rumped Swift
Bronzy Hermit
Long-tailed Hermit
Little Hermit

Blue-chested Hummingbird
Red-footed Plumeleteer
Black-throated Trogon
Belted Kingfisher
Collared Aracari
Black-cheeked Woodpecker
Plain-brown Woodcreeper
Buff-throated Woodcreeper
Fasciated Antshrike
Checker-throated Antwren
Dusky Antbird
Ochre-bellied Flycatcher
Black-headed Tody-Flycatcher
Long-tailed Tyrant
Dusky-capped Flycatcher
Snowy Cotinga
Gray-breasted Martin
Band-backed Wren
Canebrake Wren
Tropical Gnatcatcher
Yellow-throated Vireo
Tennessee Warbler
Bay-breasted Warbler
Northern Waterthrush
Olive-crowned Yellowthroat
Golden-hooded Tanager
Yellow-crowned Euphonia
White-shouldered Tanager
Sulphur-rumped Tanager
Red-throated Ant-Tanager
Crimson-collared Tanager
Black-headed Saltator
Blue-black Grosbeak

Rufous-tailed Hummingbird
Violaceous Trogon
Ringed Kingfisher
Green Kingfisher
Keel-billed Toucan
Lineated Woodpecker
Barred Woodcreeper
Streak-headed Woodcreeper
Slaty Antshrike
Dot-winged Antwren
Chestnut-backed Antbird
Common Tody-Flycatcher
Tropical Pewee
Bright-rumped Attila
Masked Tityra
White-collared Manakin
S. Rough-winged Swallow
Black-throated Wren
Long-billed Gnatwren
Clay-colored Thrush
Lesser Greenlet
Chestnut-sided Warbler
Prothonotary Warbler
Kentucky Warbler
Bananaquit
Red-legged Honeycreeper
Olive-backed Euphonia
Tawny-crested Tanager
White-lined Tanager
Summer Tanager
Scarlet-rumped Tanager
Rose-breasted Grosbeak
Black-striped Sparrow

Blue-black Grassquit
White-collared Seedeater
Giant Cowbird
Orchard Oriole
Montezuma Oropendola
Variable Seedeater
Thick-billed Seed-Finch
Black-cowled Oriole
Northern Oriole
Chestnut-headed Oropendola

Tortuguero National Park

This national park is popular with nature tourists for its nesting sea turtles and good birding. Unfortunately access is still limited following damage to the inland canal in the 1991 earthquake. Birding and the jungle experience might make a tour worthwhile, though there are few species that cannot be seen more easily elsewhere in Costa Rica. A boat trip might produce Sungrebe, Green & Rufous Kingfisher, and Rufescent Tiger-Heron.

Tours start at about $150 for three days/two nights. See any travel agent in San José for details and current schedules.

Suggested Itineraries

The following are possible two- and three-week itineraries for the first-time visitor to Costa Rica. They are intended only as a guideline; as mentioned under those locations, schedule Finca La Selva and any excursions to Tortuguero or Corcovado first and arrange the rest of your trip around availability at those locations.

Locations are suggested for accommodation assuming you wish to stay in tourist-class hotels. Those willing to camp or use a poorer standard of accommodation will obviously have more flexibility.

Two Week Itinerary

Day 1: Arrive San José. Braulio Carrillo in p.m. if time. Night in SJO.
Day 2: Tapantí. Night SJO.
Day 3: Braulio Carrillo. Night in SJO.
Day 4: Volcán Poás a.m. (Avoid weekends.) Night Liberia
Day 5: Santa Rosa National Park. Night Liberia.
Day 6: Palo Verde National Park. Night Jacó or Tárcoles.
Day 7: Carara Biological Reserve & Tárcoles. Night in Jacó.
Day 8: Carara Biological Reserve & Tárcoles. Night in SJO.
Day 9: Virgen del Socorro. Night at La Selva.
Day 10: La Selva. Night at La Selva.
Day 11: La Selva. Night at Cahuita.
Day 12: Cahuita. Upper Braulio Carrillo p.m. Night in SJO.
Day 13: Cerro de la Muerte. Night in SJO.
Day 14: Braulio in a.m. Depart SJO.

Three Week Itinerary

Days 1-6 as above.
Day 7: Monteverde. Night in Monteverde.
Day 8: Monteverde. Night in Jacó or Tárcoles.
Day 9: Carara Biological Reserve. Night in Jacó.
Day 10: Carara Biological Reserve. Night in SJO.
Day 11: Cerro de la Muerte a.m. Night in San Vito.
Day 12: San Vito area. Night in San Vito.
Day 13: San Vito area. Night in Golfito if visiting Corcovado.
Day 14: Corcovado. (Add extra day at Carara if not visiting Corcovado.)
Day 15: Corcovado. (Add day at Cahuita if not visiting Corcovado.)
Day 16: Corcovado. Return to SJO.
Day 17: Virgen del Socorro. Night at La Selva.
Day 18: La Selva. Night at La Selva.
Day 19: La Selva. Night at Cahuita.
Day 20: Cahuita. Upper Braulio Carrillo p.m. Night in SJO.
Day 21: Braulio Carrillo in a.m. or depart SJO.

Regional Specialties

Costa Rica and Panama are an important center of avian endemism, with most interesting species in the highlands. Several others are restricted to the band of lowland forest (what's left of it) in the lowlands of the Pacific slope, while a few more are restricted to the Atlantic lowlands.

This list is intended to give an idea of what areas will produce the most endemics and as such will not be of as much interest to the first-time visitor to the Neotropics. Species restricted to Darién and adjacent Colombia or Isla de Cocos are not included.

Names and taxonomy follow the AOU Checklist (1983). Much locality data come from *Birds of Costa Rica* and *Birds of Panama.*

Black-breasted Wood-Quail	Foothills, Monteverde
Chiriquí Quail-Dove	Foothills both slopes
Buff-fronted Quail-Dove	Highlands generally,
Sulphur-winged Parakeet	Higher parts Talamanca
Red-fronted Parrotlet	Caribbean side Talamanca
Bare-shanked Screech-Owl	Highlands generally
White-crested Coquette	S. Pacific foothills
Fiery-throated Hummingbird	Highest mountains, common Cerro de la Muerte
Snowy-breasted Hummingbird	SW lowlands
Mangrove Hummingbird	Pacific coast mangroves
Black-bellied Hummingbird	Foothills of SW
White-tailed Emerald	San Vito
Coppery-headed Emerald	Readily seen Monteverde
Snowcap	Caribbean foothills and adjacent lowlands
White-bellied Mountain-gem	Caribbean foothills
Purple-throated Mountain-gem	Common highlands
White-throated Mountain-gem	Talamanca
Magenta-throated Woodstar	Highlands
Volcano Hummingbird	Common highest areas, Cerro de la Muerte

Glow-throated Hummingbird	Cerro Flores, Chiriquí
Scintillant Hummingbird	Highlands, not rare
Baird's Trogon	Common Carara, Corcovado
Lattice-tailed Trogon	Caribbean foothills, Braulio
Prong-billed Barbet	Easily seen Tapantí, Monteverde
Ruddy Treerunner	Highlands
Streak-breasted Treehunter	Highlands, Monteverde
Black-hooded Antshrike	Common Carara, Corcovado
Streak-crowned Antvireo	N Caribbean lowlands
Silvery-fronted Tapaculo	Difficult to see but widespread highest elevations.
Orange-collared Manakin	Pacific lowlands
Gray-headed Manakin	Local Caribbean lowlands
Turquoise Cotinga	S. Pacific lowlands
Snowy Cotinga	Caribbean lowlands
Yellow-billed Cotinga	Pacific lowlands, mangroves
Bare-necked Umbrellabird	Local Caribbean foothills
Tawny-chested Flycatcher	Local Caribbean lowlands, foothills
Black-capped Flycatcher	High, open country
Dark Pewee	Common highlands
Ochraceous Pewee	Local higher parts Talamanca
Silvery-throated Jay	Cordillera de Talamanca
Stripe-breasted Wren	Common Caribbean lowlands
Black-bellied Wren	SW lowlands
Black-throated Wren	Caribbean lowlands
Riverside Wren	Common Carara, Corcovado
Ochraceous Wren	Common highlands
Timberline Wren	Common above timberline, Cerro de la Muerte
Sooty Thrush	Common Cerro de la Muerte
Black-billed Nightingale-Thrush	Common Monteverde etc., difficult to see
Black-faced Solitaire	Highlands, also difficult to see
Long-tailed Silky-Flycatcher	Poás, Cerro de la Muerte
Black-and-yellow Silky-Flycatcher	Common highest areas
Yellow-winged Vireo	Higher parts of S Cordilleras

Flame-throated Warbler	Readily seen highlands
Collared Whitestart	Common highlands
Black-cheeked Warbler	Cerro de la Muerte
Wrenthrush (Zeledonia)	Elfin forest zone, hard to see
Golden-browed Chlorophonia	Readily seen Tapantí
Tawny-capped Euphonia	Common Caribbean foothills
Yellow-crowned Euphonia	Caribbean lowlands
Spot-crowned Euphonia	Pacific lowlands
Spangle-cheeked Tanager	Common Monteverde, Tapantí
Blue-and-gold Tanager	Caribbean foothills
White-throated Shrike-Tanager	Caribbean foothills
Sulphur-rumped Tanager	S. Caribbean slope
Black-and-yellow Tanager	Caribbean foothills
Sooty-capped Bush-Tanager	Common highest areas
Black-cheeked Ant-Tanager	Golfo Dulce lowlands only
Black-thighed Grosbeak	Highlands
Large-footed Finch	Highlands, Braulio Carrillo
Yellow-green Finch	Chiriquí and Veraguas only
Yellow-thighed Finch	Common highest areas
Black-headed Brush-Finch	San Vito
Sooty-faced Finch	Virgen del Socorro, Braulio
Peg-billed Finch	Cerro de la Muerte
Volcano Junco	V. Irazú, Cerro de la Muerte
Nicaraguan Grackle	Río Frio, Caño Negro

Index of Locations

Index of Bird Species

Also from Cinclus Publications

Birds of Oregon: Status and Distribution

By Jeff Gilligan et. al. 1994

A complete annotated checklist of the birds of Oregon, with coverage of all 477 species known for the state up to July of 1994. Details of Oregon's geography and ornithological history round out this first complete treatment of the state's avifauna in more than 40 years.

ISBN 0-9637765-1-7 350 pp. paper $24.95

Site Guides: Costa Rica

A Guide to the Best Birding Locations

By Dennis Rogers 1994

Extensive coverage of the best birdwatching sites in Costa Rica with information on other aspects of visiting that country. Directions and a list of species likely to be seen are included for each location.

Complete index.

ISBN 0-9637765-2-5 90 pp. paper $14.50

Site Guides: Venezuela

A Guide to thc Bcst Birding Locations

By Dennis Rogers 1993

Coverage of 20 prime birding locations in all parts of the country, with possible species for each. A complete checklist of all 1350 species in Venezuela is included, along with an index of all species mentioned in the text.

ISBN 0-9637765-0-9 48 p. 8½X11 spiral $14.50

Site Guides: La Ruta Maya

A Guide to the Best Birding Locations in The Yucatan, Belize, Guatemala, Honduras, and El Salvador.

By Dennis Rogers 1994

Birding guide to the former empire of the Maya, with information on visiting each country involved and details and species lists for each specific site.

ISBN 0-9637765-3-3 54 p. paper $8.95

A Bird Finding Guide to Alaska

By Nick Lethaby 1994

Guide to 22 well-known sites, with details on planning your trip and 14 maps. An annotated list of Alaska specialties and index are included.

ISBN 0-9637765-9-2 152 p. paper $14.95

Order Form

Title	Copies	@	subtotal
Birds of Oregon	___	$24.95	____
Site Guides: Costa Rica	___	$14.50	____
Site Guides: Venezuela	___	$14.50	____
Site Guides: La Ruta Maya	___	$8.95	____
A Bird Finding Guide to Alaska	___	$14.95	____
Shipping and Handling			____

Add $2 for first book, $1 for each additional title.

Total _____

Make checks payable to:

Cinclus Publications
Box 284
McMinnville, OR, 97128